THE SWORD OF THE SPIRIT

HOW GOD'S WORD CHANGES LIVES

By Kelly Malone

ISBN-10: 0-9825719-0-9
ISBN-13: 978-0-9825719-0-3

Printed in the United States of America

Cover Design by Grant Cochran
Cover Photo of Author by Jenny Blair

Gratefully dedicated to
John W. Shepard, Jr.
and
James Leo Garrett, Jr.,

Trusted teachers, mentors and friends
Who taught me by their example
What it means to follow
Our Lord Jesus Christ

CONTENTS

ACKNOWLEDGEMENTS

The Sword of the Spirit was written on the journey through a life of change. There are so many people that contributed to the completion of this work that I hesitate to mention any, lest I leave out many to whom I owe a debt of gratitude.

This journey began in 1999-2000, when my family and I were on a year's furlough from our mission work in Japan, living in a house provided to us by Grace Baptist Church in Oxford, Alabama. During that year, Dr. Timothy George, the dean of the Beeson Divinity School at Samford University in Birmingham, graciously extended the invitation for me to be a visiting scholar at his institution. Much of the preliminary research which led to the writing of the initial manuscript that eventually became *The Sword of the Spirit* occurred during that time.

Colleagues in mission in Japan, both missionaries and national believers committed to follow Christ and to make disciples, encouraged me to think both biblically and practically about what is at stake in the fulfillment of the Great Commission.

Discussions with faculty at the various institutions where I have taught—Seinan Jo Gakuin College, Kitakyushu, Japan, Tokyo Baptist Seminary and Christian Leadership

Training Center, both in Tokyo, and Southwest Baptist University, Bolivar, Missouri—have helped me to continue to refine my thinking in this area.

I also must express thanks to David Phillips, Erin Amundson and the other fine folks at Missional Press—without your willingness to take this project on it would have never reached completion. To this I must add a word of appreciate to Grant Cochran, an extraordinary graphic artist and fellow faculty member at Southwest Baptist University, whose skills produced the cover. Great job Grant!

Finally, I am so thankful to Molly, Maggie and Kevin, my wonderful family who, apart from salvation, are God's greatest work of grace in my life. God continues to use you to challenge me to become more like Jesus. Thanks for your continual encouragement. You allowed me time to write and to encourage me to complete the task with the not so subtle question, "Are you done yet?" I thank God at every remembrance of you!

While credit for the quality of this work goes to these and many others, I take full responsibility for any weaknesses, omissions and errors. No human work is perfect, but thanks be to our Lord Jesus Christ, that His grace is perfected in our weakness. All glory, honor and praise are due to Him.

Kelly Malone
Bolivar, Missouri
September 2009

PROLOGUE

TAKING UP THE SPIRIT'S SWORD

People tend to base their spiritual hope on their own strengths and abilities. To say, "While we are saved by the blood of Jesus, real spiritual change comes by means of our own toil and sweat." We encourage this tendency when we explain what *people must do* in a way that nullifies God's role in the process. For example, we tell people that if they believe in Jesus and say the sinner's prayer they will be saved. As a result, many people believe that these human actions, apart from any intervention on God's part, can save a person from sin, death and hell. This is more like belief in magic than it is a biblical understanding of salvation by God's grace through faith (Eph. 6:10). It is the work of God's Spirit in us that saves from sin and brings new life; no human activity can save.

The same problem occurs in many popular presentations of spiritual growth. People are told, "Go to church, read the Bible, pray, witness, serve others, and you will grow to be like Christ." The problem with this assertion is that a person can follow through with all these activities and never even have a personal relationship with Jesus Christ. The disciple's life is not primarily a matter of human activity; it is a life lived out in relationship to Jesus. We learn to be like Jesus by following Him; we develop the character of Christ through obedience to His Word.

The decision to follow Christ occurs within the context God's struggle against Satan, which has raged from the time of Satan's fall until the present and encompasses the whole created order. Every dimension of evil in the present world, "racism, totalitarianism, terrorism, torture, war, scientism, depersonalizing technocracy, waste and pollution," is drawn into this cosmic struggle between good and evil.[1] Paul writes,

> Our struggle is not against flesh and blood, but against the rulers, against the authorities, against the powers of this dark world, and against the spiritual forces of evil in the heavenly realms (Eph. 6:12).

"Struggle" here does not elude anything like modern warfare in which pilots of unmanned aircraft sit in cubicles ten thousand miles away from any threat of danger and unleash their savagery on unsuspecting enemies. Rather, the picture is of ancient warriors locked together in bloody hand-to-hand combat.[2] There is a real risk involved in the decision to follow Christ. We are going to get our hands dirty; we are going to get hurt. Our participation necessitates "effort, stamina and . . . spiritual fitness" for this grueling struggle which continues as long as our life in the present world.[3]

The primary contention in this struggle is between God's truth and Satan's lies. The devil attempts to deceive us in order to separate us from God through a life of sin.[4] God provides us with "mighty power" through His armor so that we can resist the devil's schemes (Eph. 6:10-11). To put on the "full armor of God" (Eph. 6:13) is to clothe ourselves in the protection God has provided for us in Jesus Christ, to live in His strength, and to allow Him to be our defense.[5]

Every piece of God's armor in some way points to our position in relationship to Jesus Christ. The belt and breastplate (Eph. 6:14) are the truth and righteousness of Christ who protects us from Satanic attack. The shoes of the "gospel of peace" (Eph. 6:15) prepare us to advance with confidence in the face of the enemy. The shield which protects us from the "flaming arrows of the evil one" (Eph. 6:16) is our faith in Christ. Bryan Zacharias writes that "this faith is not simply mental assent to the truth." It is, rather, "justifying faith" which "is that act by which the whole person trusts wholly upon the whole Christ for pardon from sin and eternal life." Only those that have this kind of faith in Christ are impregnable to satanic assault.[6]

When we decline our need to trust in Christ and choose to live apart from Him, we open ourselves up to Satan's onslaught. This is one of the problems with any human quest for spiritual fulfillment apart from Christ: any shield that we construct for our own self-defense will be shot through with holes.

"The Christian warrior wears the helmet of salvation (Eph. 6:17) in the sense that he is the receiver and possessor of deliverance, clothed and armed in the victory of his Head, Jesus Christ."[7] The Puritan Richard Alleine has written,

> Salvation must be your helmet, that is, your hope . . . which has salvation as its object. This hope is an assured expectation of victory and glory. The helmet secures the head. A good hope of salvation, well founded, will be the means of keeping the soul from being defiled by sin and of comforting the soul and keeping it from being troubled and tormented by Satan. Good hope keeps the Christian trusting in God and rejoicing in Him.[8]

Finally, we come to the "sword of the Spirit, which is the word of God" (Eph. 6:17). The Greek word *rhema* translated "word" refers literally to a "verbal utterance." This is best understood as the proclamation of God's Word, centered in the message of Christ, under the guidance of the Holy Spirit. In Romans 10:8, 17, Paul states explicitly that the "word (*rhema*) of Christ" is preached in order to bring about the salvation of the hearer. God's Spirit uses our proclamation of the good news of Jesus Christ to bring about the acceptance of truth, conviction of sin, and trust in Christ that result in spiritual transformation.[9]

God desires to conform us to the image of His Son, Jesus Christ. When this type of change occurs, it is the result of a divine-human process, initiated by God but worked out in the human sphere as we respond to God's leadership. It is God's Spirit at work in us who brings about this change through the application of God's Word in our lives. This is why Paul writes,

> We have not received the spirit of the world but the Spirit who is from God, that we may understand what God has freely given to us. This is what we speak, not in words taught us by human wisdom but in words taught by the Spirit, expressing spiritual truths in spiritual words (1 Cor. 2:12-13).

Paul distinguishes between the "spirit of the world," or Satan, who is the source of "human wisdom" and the "Spirit who is from God" who teaches us "spiritual truths." Human wisdom does not refer to all human pursuit of knowledge, but rather to the human desire to explain truth apart from the God who has revealed Himself to us in Jesus Christ. This version of truth, often referred to as secular humanism, is a dead end because it fails to address the deepest needs of human existence: the search for meaning, purpose and eternal relevance. It does not answer the all-important questions, "Why are we here?" and, "What difference will it make that we have been here?" However, God has given us the answer to these questions in the form of "spiritual truths" taught by His Spirit.

This book is about how God's Spirit transforms us into the likeness of God's Son by helping us to understand and apply God's Word, so that we can know "why we are here" and live accordingly. The first section of the book, "God's Word in the Transformed Life," deals with the individual transformation process. It begins by explaining the spiritual condition that we are in apart from God's transforming work, fallen individuals in a world that has been deceived and corrupted by Satan. The second chapter deals with the most essential ingredient in a transformed life—trust in Christ that enables us to follow Him, even when the world and other people tell us not to. The third chapter is about the goal of discipleship, which is to become like Christ.

The second section of *The Sword of the Spirit,* "God's Word in His Mission," deals with how God's Word brings about change on the corporate level. Chapter four is about the multifaceted nature of the Great Commission Jesus has given to His followers, to "make disciples of all nations" (Matt. 28:19). Chapter five uses the account of the early church in Acts to remind us that proclamation of the gospel begins with, but far exceeds evangelism. The final chapter is about how believers, in the context of Christian community, can encourage one another to live out the implications of God's Word under the leadership of the Holy Spirit.

My prayer is that this book will enable you to experience the life-changing power of God's Word under the leadership of God's Spirit, to God's glory!

PART ONE

GOD'S WORD IN THE TRANSFORMED LIFE

"The Word became flesh and made his dwelling among us. We have seen his glory, the glory of the One and Only, who came from the Father, full of grace and truth."
John 1:14

"God was reconciling the world to himself in Christ, not counting men's sins against them. And he has committed to us the message of reconciliation."
2 Corinthians 5:19

God made a personal investment in our lives. He gave His own Son, Jesus Christ, who took the form of a man so that we could see God's love and experience God's transforming power through Him.

God's Word calls us to move beyond belief in propositional truth to place our personal trust in Jesus Christ. Faith in Christ frees us from the results of living in a darkened world, influenced by Satan, enslaved to sin and encumbered with death.

This freedom does not come easily. It comes as a result of following Jesus.

CHAPTER ONE

WHAT'S WRONG WITH GOD'S WORLD AND WHAT HE'S DOING ABOUT IT

Response to God's call to international missions necessitates going home to a place we have never lived, befriending those we do not know, experiencing a culture that is distant from our own, and speaking a language that is different from what we learned as a child. Although I served as a missionary for over fifteen years, I did not travel widely. I spent the whole time serving in Japan which has now become as familiar to me as the small town in east Texas where I grew up. Yet, I distinctly remember experiencing what it felt like to go home to a new place.

In 1984, I had the opportunity to serve for six months as a student missionary in Nagasaki, Japan. This was my first opportunity to serve overseas. I had been called to missions in Japan two years before during my freshman year in college, had studied the Japanese language for one and a half years, and was excited to finally step foot in the place where I intended to plant my life. Missionaries met me at the airport in Fukuoka and took me to their house where I spent my first night and saw my first morning in Japan. Then they put me on the train for the two hour ride to Nagasaki. As I sat on the train it struck me for the first time how far I was from east Texas. The rice fields, tiled-roof houses, and groves of bamboo looked very different from the wheat fields I was used to. And although I had studied Japanese, I was not at all confident that I could communicate in a language that sounded different from the familiar Texas drawl. The speed was much faster than what I had heard in the classroom in Waco. Fear struck me when I thought, "What if I try to speak *in Japanese* and no one understands me?"

The greatest struggle I faced during those six months turned out to be spiritual rather than cultural. I learned to deal with language limitations, cultural misunderstandings, homesickness and loneliness that are common experiences for those involved in cross-cultural ministry. But I continued to struggle with the rejection of the gospel. Sometimes I felt like the words that I was saying were falling on deaf ears. I should not have been surprised. Jesus told His followers that some would not welcome them when they went out to preach his Word (Luke 10:10). Jesus prayed for us because He knew the world would reject us just as it rejected Him (John 17:14).

Jesus knows about rejection firsthand. He came to "his own" (John 1:11). In the original Greek, the description is of a ruler who returned to "his own home" and "his own people."[1] Jesus had every right to expect a hero's welcome for He came, not as a foreign conqueror, but as the King returning to claim

His throne.[2] The proper response to Jesus' coming should have been "that at the name of Jesus every knee should bow, in heaven and on earth and under the earth, and every tongue confess that Jesus Christ is Lord, to the glory of God the Father" (Phil. 2:10-11).

The world does not belong to Jesus by right of conquest. It belongs to him by right of creation. This is because "through him all things we made; and without him nothing was made that has been made" (John 1:3). Not only were "all things . . . created by him," but they were also created "for him" (Col. 1:16). Jesus came "to fulfill what He began long ago when He said, "Let Us create . . ." At long last, when everything was ready, the Word, the Son of God, Jesus Christ, came to that

> which by all rights belonged to Him. After all, He made it. He holds it together. It is all for Him. He came to complete what He intended millennia before when He made the world, hung the stars in space, and caused the planets around the sun to spin. He came to finish what He planned when He separated the water from the land and filled both of them with life.[3]

Jesus did not come as a foreigner to a strange land. The world rightfully belonged to Him, but "his own did not receive him" (John 1:12). There was no hero's welcome for the coming King. Rather, He was "rejected" by the very ones who should have welcomed Him. This included not only the people of Israel who had a special covenant relationship with God, but also all of the peoples of the world. We have all been created by Him for His glory.[4] But the people of every nation, tribe, culture and language have "despised" and "rejected" Him (Isaiah 53:3).

Jesus was not surprised by this rejection. The world to which Jesus came had long been under the rule of another. In John's Gospel, Satan is repeatedly described as the "prince of this world" (12:31; 14:30; 16:11). Elsewhere in the New Testament we read that Satan is the "god of this age" (2 Cor. 4:4) and the "ruler of the kingdom of the air, the spirit who is now at work in those who are disobedient" (Eph. 2:2). "The whole world is under the control of the evil one" (1 John 5:19). That is, although the world rightfully belongs to Jesus, Satan "exercises controlling influence over it."[5]

This spiritual conflict between Jesus and Satan forms the background for understanding what this book is about. It is within this context that we come to understand both the power of the Word of God and why it is essential for mission. The rejection of Jesus provides a basis for understanding why those we share the gospel with reject us and our message. People reject the gospel because they are in spiritual bondage. Although Jesus has come to set people free (John 8:32), they reject Him, choosing instead to remain enslaved to sin and death. The only possible explanation for this circumstance is that Satan "has blinded the minds of unbelievers, so that they cannot see the light of the gospel of the glory of Christ" (2 Cor. 4:4). In this sightless state, they confuse bondage for freedom, evil for good, and darkness for light. They choose to stay on the dark road that leads to death rather than turn to the way of light that leads to eternal life.

This also explains why it is imperative for us to continue to share God's Word. It is only through God's Word that people experience the "truth" which is able to set them "free" (John 8:32). Without this truth there is only bondage, darkness, sin and death. But in the light of the gospel's truth, there is eternal life. So it is essential for us to bring the power of God's Word to bear upon our darkened world.

In the final analysis, Satan is unable to prevent his own defeat. But this does not mean that he is willing to give up without a fight. He is committed to resisting the advance of God's kingdom at all costs. Satan is not above using lying, torture, and every manner of vice in the service of his cause. As a matter of fact, he is committed to it. Satan is the father of evil. He will lie, steal, kill and destroy to prevent people from experiencing new life through a relationship with Jesus Christ.

This chapter deals with the spiritual condition of the world in which we now live. The world fell under Satan's domination long ago. As a result, the influence of Satan and evil spirits in the world is pervasive, but not definitive. In other words, Satan and his forces are able to exercise influence and some degree of control in our world. But this influence and control are limited. They are limited because God has ultimate power and authority over our world. Satan's authority also is limited by the degree to which *we* allow him to control our lives.

Jesus came to make things right. He came to set people free from the power of Satan and to bring them into God's family as His children. Jesus could do this because He is the Word of God. Jesus is the Word who took on human flesh (John 1:14) to bring freedom from the bondage of sin that leads to death (Rom. 6:23).

How the World Got This Way

When the world was created God "saw all that he had made, and it was very good" (Gen. 1:31). This was the world as God meant for it to be. There was neither envy nor pride, neither lust nor selfish desires. There was no famine or illness. There was no death. Human beings lived in a paradise in which all was right with God. In this perfect world "God's invisible qualities—his eternal power and divine nature" (Rom. 1:20) were clearly seen. Human beings were accorded a place of "glory and honor" as rulers over all the "works" of God's "hands" (Ps. 8:5, 6; Gen. 1:28-30).

Many people believe that this description of the world in the first two chapters of Genesis is myth. This is not only because they deny God's creative activity. It is also because thoughts of paradise in the past are crowded out by realities of the present. Standing in midst of the evil and corruption of our present existence, they cannot see the world as it once was. Questions crying out for answers fill our souls. Why do innocent children in Africa perish from AIDS? Why are half a million people in South Asia swept into eternity suddenly by a tsunami on a silent Sunday morning? Why do guns and bombs maim and destroy lives in the Middle East? Why do heart disease and cancer take a terrible toll on both the victims and their families? Why do bad things happen to good and bad people alike? How did this perfect world which God created for His glory become the seemingly God-forsaken place where we suffer for a few short years before we die?

The Bible tells us that everything that exists, other than God himself, was created by God. God created the world through His Word (John 1:3), who later took on human form in the person of Jesus Christ (John 1:14). This includes not only the material universe, such as stars and planets, animals and plants, but also the spiritual universe as well. "For by him all things were created: things in heaven and on earth, visible and invisible, whether thrones or powers or rulers or authorities" (Col. 1:16).

When Jesus came into the world which was "his own" (John 1:11), this included spiritual beings as well. They belong to Him. The writer of Hebrews writes regarding the Son of God, "Let all the angels worship him" (1:6). The book of Revelation repeatedly pictures the angels participating in the worship of God's Son (4:8; 5:11-12; 7:11-12). Just as God created us to bear witness to His glory on earth, He created the angels to bear witness to His glory in the heavens.[6]

Lucifer, literally "son of the dawn" (Isa. 14:11), was one of these angels created by God's Son for his glory. Ezekiel describes Lucifer as God originally created and intended him to be:[7]

> You were the model of perfection, full of wisdom and perfect in beauty. . . . You were anointed as a guardian cherub, for so I ordained you. You were on the holy mount of God; you walked among the fiery stones. You were blameless in your ways from the day you were created till wickedness was found in you (Ezek. 28:12, 14-15).

Lucifer was appointed by God to serve as a "guardian." Although it is not explicit Ezekiel 28, this probably means that Lucifer's responsibility was to oversee and take care of God's affairs on earth. This would explain at least one reason why Jesus refers to Satan as the "prince of this world" (12:31; 14:30; 16:11). It may be that God created hierarchies of angels with certain assigned spheres of authority within His created order.[8] This could explain the references to "thrones, powers, rulers and authorities" in the New Testament (Eph. 6:12; Col. 1:16). Lucifer was a high ranking angel who was in position to produce the "greatest good" on earth if he chose to obey God, but he also had the capacity for great evil if he chose disobedience.[9] But Lucifer was not satisfied with his role as ruler of a small blue planet in one corner of the universe. Lucifer wanted it all! His "heart became proud" and "corrupted" (Ezek. 28:17). Refusing to submit to the will of the one true God, Lucifer said, "I am god" (Ezek. 28:9). He said, "I will ascend to heaven; I will raise my throne above the stars of God. . . . I will make myself like the Most High" (Isa. 14:13, 14).

Lucifer's attempt to become like god led to cosmic cataclysm. His attempted rebellion was defeated and he was forced to leave heaven. When Lucifer fell he took legions of angels with him. This prince of angels became Satan, the ruler of evil spirits. Satan's sin "desecrated" what God had created for His worship and glory (Ezek. 28:18). The earth, once teaming with life, became a place of corruption and death (Isa. 14:15-20). Spiritual beings created to glorify God became evil forces in a state of hostile rebellion against God. Evil came as a "tragic intrusion into God's otherwise good creation."[10]

In Genesis 3, Satan's intention in was to draw human beings into his rebellion against God. Although Genesis 3 does not mention Satan by name, Revelation 12:9 refers to "that ancient serpent called the devil or Satan, who leads the whole world astray." Satan's purpose was to dupe Eve and Adam into submitting to his evil plan.[11]

At first, Satan's approach was indirect. He began by raising doubts of the truthfulness of God's Word. The serpent asked Eve, "Did God really say, 'You must not eat from any tree in the garden?" (Gen. 3:1). The answer to this question, of course, was no. Eve replied, "We may eat fruit from the trees in the garden . . . [but not] from the tree in the middle of the garden, and you must not touch it, or you will die" (Gen. 3:2, 3). Eve was correct that God told them not to eat from the tree in the middle of the garden (Gen. 2:17), but God never told Adam and Eve not to *touch* the fruit.

Adam and Eve must have added this extra rule in order to distance themselves from temptation. Perhaps the fruit of this tree looked especially wonderful so Adam and Eve realized if they came near enough to even touch the fruit they could not keep from eating it. They reasoned, "If we cannot eat the fruit it is better not to even touch it." Even in the Garden of Eden where continual direct contact with God was available, people decided to use their own ingenuity and strength in order to maintain innocence. This dependence on human ability rather than on a personal relationship with God is the essence of religion. This religious commitment did not prevent sin. Rather, it provided Satan with the opportunity he sought to turn the world upside down.

When Satan heard this extra rule made to prevent falling into evil, he knew that he had found a glitch in paradise—a weakness that he could use to get Eve and Adam to fall under his control. Before Satan had been subtle, but now he pressed his case by using a bold-faced lie. Satan said in direct contradiction to God's Word: "You will not surely die . . . God knows that when you eat of it . . . you will be like God" (Gen. 3:4, 5).

Satan's goal is to get people to oppose God. The name "Satan" means "adversary." He is God's adversary who stands in opposition to God's purpose for His creation.[12] Satan also is our adversary because he opposes what is best for human beings. Satan told Adam and Eve that if they would disregard what God said and obey Satan instead, they no longer would be mere creatures under the authority of Creator God. Rather, they would become gods themselves! No longer under God's rule, they would decide what was right and wrong (Gen. 3:5).

Satan not only wanted to convince Eve and Adam to no longer worship and serve God. Satan wanted them to worship him.[13] To accomplish this, Satan had to get people to believe God had not been totally honest with them. God had told them a half-truth so that He could keep them in line. God did not want them to reach their full potential because He was selfish--He wanted to be the only "God" in paradise. Now Satan was telling them the "real truth" that would enable them to reach their true "divine" destiny.[14]

Our first ancestors did not know that Satan is the one "who holds the power of death" (Heb. 2:14). Satan exercises this power through the lie, which he uses for temptation, which bears the fruit of sin, which results in death (Jas. 1:13; Rom. 6:23). In turning their backs on God, Eve and Adam not only substituted a lie for the truth. They also substituted disobedience for obedience, rebellion for faithfulness, selfishness for service, sin for righteousness, evil for good, and death for life.

The Bible tells us the whole world was cursed when Adam and Eve sinned (Gen. 3:17-19). The "whole creation has been groaning" as it awaits "redemption" (Rom. 8:22, 23). It has become subject to "bondage and decay" because it is controlled by spiritual forces that oppose the One who created the universe and gave us life. The place which God once created for His glory has become estranged from Him. This separation from the source of life results not only in sin and evil, but also in sickness, suffering and death.[15]

This is why the world in which we live seems like such a God-forsaken place. The problem is not that God has forsaken the world. The problem is that the world, falling into Satan's grasp, has turned its back on God and forsaken Him. As a result of our desire to decide good and evil for ourselves, we have turned aside from good and gone down the path towards evil (Isa. 53:6).

The world, no longer under the rule of the benevolent Creator, groans under the curse of a malevolent evil spirit. This is why there is hatred, prejudice and bigotry, theft and murder, terrorism and war. This is why nature erupts into storms, disaster and pestilence. This is why both evil men and innocent children die.

But, this is also why Jesus came.

Why Jesus Came

The Gospels tell us that Jesus healed a man who was blind and mute due to the influence of an evil spirit (Matt. 12:22; Luke 11:14). Although some contemporary readers may dismiss this story as mythology or try to explain it away in terms of modern psychology,[16] the biblical writers, the people in the story and Jesus all believed the deaf and mute man was under the influence of an evil spirit. They believed evil spirits could bring about physical results, in this case causing a man to be deaf and mute. Jesus healed the man by casting out the evil spirit (Luke 11:14).

When the Pharisees heard about Jesus casting out the evil spirit, they responded, "It is only by Beelzebub, the prince of demons, that this fellow drives out demons" (Matt. 12:24). *Beel* is an Aramaic term meaning "lord" or "god." It is closely related to the Canaanite word *Baal* used in the Old Testament to describe the indigenous gods worshiped by the peoples that occupied Canaan when the Israelites entered the land, and which many Hebrews subsequently worshiped as well. In the Old Testament, the *Baals* always are described as idols and false gods. The name *Beelzebub* most likely means "lord of the dwelling." By using this expression the Jewish religious leaders equated the gods of other nations with evil spirits, inferred that Satan is the one who commands these spirits, and asserted that Jesus carried out His work in allegiance to Satan as well.[17]

Many people think all religions and belief systems point to the same ultimate reality. However, Jesus did not contradict the Pharisees' statement about the relationship between Satan and the gods of other religions. Jesus seems to be indicating that the other gods which people serve are part of the system Satan uses to bind people in order to prevent them from realizing their potential as persons created in the image of God.

Jesus did point out a self-contradiction inherent in the Pharisees' argument. He said Satan would not destroy his own kingdom by fighting against himself (Luke 11:17-18). Then He mentioned that the Pharisees' followers also exorcised demons. If Jesus did this by Satan's power, what power did they use? (Luke 11:19). It was inconsistent to condemn Jesus for casting out an evil spirit when the Pharisees' own disciples did the same kind of activity.[18]

Then Jesus focused on the true nature of His relationship to the kingdom of Satan—as an outsider, an intruder, and One who has come to "bind Satan" in order to set his "possessions" free (Matt. 12:29). Jesus pointed to the real source of His authority over the evil spirit as the "finger of God" (Luke 11:20) or, the "Spirit of God" (Matt. 12:28). God's hand was at work in Jesus Christ. The authority Jesus had to overcome evil spirits was the authority of God Himself. So casting out the evil spirit was evidence of the intrusion of God's kingdom into Satan's domain.[19]

Jesus used the parable of the strongman (Matt. 12:29; Mark 3:27; Luke 11:21-22) to emphasize this point. The strongman is a soldier, fully armed and armored, ready for conflict.[20] But One who is stronger breaks into the strongman's house and binds him so that he is unable to defend himself. Then He plunders the strongman's house. In this story the strongman is Satan and the stronger One who "attacks and overpowers him" (Luke 11:22) is Jesus. Jesus came to bind Satan in order to liberate those who are under his control.[21] Those who were once Satan's "possessions" are now the "property of Christ."[22]

The purpose of Jesus' mission was to free God's creation from the rule of Satan. While this theme runs throughout the New Testament, it is easy to miss because it usually is not explicitly stated. The New Testament emphasizes the freedom which Christ brings from the results of Satan's rule, in particular sin, alienation and death by stating positively God's gifts of forgiveness of sin, restored relationships with God and other people, and eternal life. These gifts are intended for the "whole world" (1 John 2:2). However, only believers in Christ receive them (John 3:16; Rom. 10:4, 13). This is why it is essential for people to hear and believe the truth about Jesus Christ. Whether or not people will have the opportunity to hear this truth is at the hub of the conflict which now rages between God and Satan.

The Truth in Conflict

In John 8, we find Jesus talking again with the Pharisees, this time about the validity of Jesus' words. The Pharisees claimed that since Jesus had no one to verify His testimony it was impossible for Jesus to prove that His words were true (John 8:13). In response, Jesus said that the veracity of His words could not be measured by human standards (8:13), and that God the Father would witness to the truth of His words (8:16, 18). This was unacceptable to Jesus' listeners who considered it blasphemy for Jesus to claim such an intimate relationship with God. Jesus told his adversaries that they were incapable of understanding the truth because they "belong to [their] father, the devil" who is "the father of lies" (John 8:43-44). The Jews, in turn, called Jesus "demon-possessed" (8:48), which was akin to calling Jesus a liar.

Both Jesus and His opponents believed in absolute truth. They also understood they had two contradictory views of truth. If Jesus' words were true, then the Pharisees words were false. And if the Pharisees' words were true, Jesus was a liar. They both could not be right. Both Jesus and the Pharisees recognized that truth and falsehood had contradictory spiritual sources. God is the source of the truth; Satan is the source of untruth. Thus the issue of truth had incredible spiritual significance for them.

Many have tried to take the question of truth off the table. I was involved in a discussion with a group of Japanese Christians on the importance of evangelism. This took place in a conservative church where people were taught that salvation comes through faith in Jesus Christ. The people I was talking with all claimed to be believers in Jesus Christ. However, they were unwilling to say that Jesus is the only way of salvation. One woman said, "I cannot say that a Muslim or a Buddhist is not saved through his or her faith." Another person said, "While we are saved through faith in Jesus, other people may be saved through something else." In essence, they were saying, "Truth is in the mind of the believer. What is true for one person may differ from what is true for another."

This kind of discussion is not limited to Japan. I have talked with Christians in the United States that hold the same basic position as these Japanese Christians. Some are members of conservative congregations where the necessity of faith in Christ for salvation is preached every Sunday. What is preached and taught as gospel truth is filtered out by people whose relativistic worldviews cause them not to impose their version of the truth on anyone else. Some say, "It does not make much difference what people believe as long as they are happy with it." Mark Heim states this issue well when he writes,

> The question is not just whether we ought to proclaim Christ. If we believe Christ is *our* Lord, we would be expected to do no less. The question is whether it is objectively *true* that Jesus Christ is the way, the truth, and the life. It is not just a matter of whether we ought to preach Christ, but of whether people ought to believe us. Is Christ the only way, the definitive truth, the abundant life?[23]

Jesus said, "You will know the truth, and the truth will set you free" (John 8:32). Jesus was saying that it really does make a difference what people believe. A belief is only as powerful as the object of that belief. There is such a thing as *the truth,* in particular *truth about God*. When people come to know this truth and entrust their lives to this truth, it has the power to free them.

Truth has the power to bring freedom because Satan uses *the lie* to hold people in bondage. Jesus said that Satan is a "liar and the father of lies." Those who believe Satan's deceptions "belong" to him (John 8:44). This does not necessarily mean demonic possession. It means that people's thoughts have been warped and twisted by Satan's influence so that, apart from God's intervention, they are incapable of correct thinking. They are unable to distinguish between truth and untruth.

One of Satan's primary tactics is to deceive people so they misunderstand who Jesus is. "The god of this age has blinded the minds of unbelievers, so that they cannot see the light of the gospel of the glory of Christ, who is the image of God" (2 Cor.4:4). As a result of spiritual blindness, those who look at Jesus fail to see God's glory. They may think He was only a Jew who lived in Palestine during the Roman Empire. Some say that His moral teachings were on such a scale that they deserve adherence by people today. Others will go so far as to say that He is *a savior,* one possible way of salvation among many viable alternatives.[24]

Three primary heresies of early Christianity were based upon "distorted images of Christ." On one hand, the *Docetists* taught that Jesus had not really taken on human form, that He only appeared to be human. On the other hand, the *Ebionites* and *Arians* insisted that Jesus was not really God. He was a spiritual being who stood as an intermediary between us and God. Finally, there were those like the *Judaizers* who said that Jesus' Atonement for our sins was not enough. We must also earn our salvation through obedience to the law.[25] These distorted views of Jesus Christ remain with us today, but we have added other heresies to our list as well: the "Rambo" Jesus, the "Santa Claus" Jesus, the "my best fan" Jesus, the "my servant" Jesus, and the "my pal" Jesus, to name only a few.[26]

God's truth has power to free people from the bondage of Satan's lie. This is because Satan's lie cannot resist God's truth.[27] In *The Wedge of Truth,* Philip Johnson points out that it is only the Word which God has spoken to us that provides the proper framework for understanding the world and our place in it, life and the purpose of life, God and our relationship with God.[28] This Word has come to us in the person of Jesus Christ. First, God created the world through Christ (John 1:2; Col. 1:16). Second, God's love for His creation has been made known to us through His Son (John 3:16; 1 John 4:9) to the extent that Jesus died on the cross for our sins (1 John 4:10). As a result, those who believe in Christ are saved from sin and death (John 3:16; Rom. 6:23; 1 John 4:4). Those who know this truth given to us in Christ will be set free (John 8:32) from the manipulative power of Satan's lies. Those who know Jesus are freed from the power of sin and death to enjoy the blessings of forgiveness and new life in Christ.

The Living Word

When proclaiming the gospel we often find ourselves in conflict with Satan, evil spirits, temptation and other manifestations of evil. Considering the influence they exert in the present world, this comes as no surprise. "For our struggle is not against flesh and blood, but against the rulers, against the authorities, against the powers of this dark world and against spiritual forces of evil in the heavenly realms" (Eph. 6:12). Jesus said, "If the world hates you, keep in mind that it hated me first" (John 15:18).

We tend to see spiritual conflict only as a result of our own weaknesses. Satan will attack us when and where we are most vulnerable. But we must also keep in mind that Jesus was tempted as a result of His obedience to God's will. Immediately after His baptism, "Jesus was led by the Spirit into the desert *to be tempted by Satan*" (Matt. 4:1, emphasis mine). Carrying out God's will inevitably brought Jesus into conflict with Satan.[29] We should expect this same kind of conflict as well. This is not because God causes us to be tempted in order for us to fall into sin. God will not do that (Jas. 1:13). Rather, God uses our weakness as an opportunity to reveal His great strength (2 Cor. 12:7-9).

In his temptation of Jesus, Satan used the same weapon that he used when he tempted Eve. Satan was so arrogant that he believed he could drive a wedge into the Trinity, separating God the Son from God the Father in the same way that he had separated human beings from God. This weapon was the lie. To paraphrase Satan's words to Jesus, "You don't need your Father. You have the power to feed yourself. Just turn this stone into bread" (Matt. 4:3; Luke 4:3). "Don't let your Father push you around and make you do things His way. You can control and manipulate God to get Him to do what you want. Make Him do it your way. Jump off this temple. If God cares about you He will have to send His angels to save you" (Matt. 4:5-6; Luke 4:9-10). "Now Jesus, you don't need your Father because I am the one with real power. I am the god of this world. So if you want to have a part in ruling this world, all you have to do is worship me" (Matt. 4:8-9; Luke 4:5-7).

Satan's three temptations were attempts to get Jesus to act on the basis of His own decision, independent of His Father's will.[30] If Satan could get Jesus to deny the Creator is the one true God, to act independently of this God,[31] and to submit to Satan's presumed authority, then he would have accomplished his purpose.

When Satan tempted Jesus, he addressed Jesus as the Son of God (Matt. 4:3; 4:5; Luke

4:3; 4:9). The translation "if you are the Son of God" in the New International Version may cause us to think that Satan was raising the question of whether or not Jesus considered Himself to be God's Son. In fact, Satan's words are better rendered, "Since you are God's Son . . ." Not only does Satan tempt ordinary people like you and me. He is so proud that he does not hesitate to tempt God Himself. We see this clearly in Satan's accusation of God in Job 1 and 2. Here, Satan's willingness to mock God and challenge His goodness shows how evil flows out of Satan's utter contempt for God's rightful authority over His creation.[32]

Jesus' responses to Satan reflected not only Jesus' divine authority, but also His total reliance upon and trust in God the Father. Jesus' trust in the Father is expressed in His words to His followers, "He who sent me is reliable, and what I have heard from him I tell the world" (John 8:26), and "Trust in God; trust also in me" (John 14:1), as well as in the final words of Jesus' prayer before He went to the cross, "Not my will, but yours be done" (Luke 22:42; cf. Matt. 26:42; Mark 14:36). This same trust in God is God's will for every person and is the key to victory over Satan.

Jesus responded to each of Satan's temptations by speaking the words of Scripture, the written Word of God. Jesus' three responses to Satan's temptations are each taken from Deuteronomy (8:3; 6:16, 13). In their original context, these verses reflect Israel's exclusive relationship with the one true God. This is particularly clear in Jesus' citation of Deuteronomy 6:13:

"Worship the Lord your God, and serve him only." The immediate context in Deuteronomy speaks of Israel's relationship with the God who has brought them out of slavery in Egypt. There was no room for the worship of other gods, especially the gods of the surrounding nations. The Old Testament teaches that these gods were evil spirits that "solicited worship under their guise as local deities" (Ps. 96:5; 106:36-38).[33] The early church also regarded idols as means that evil spirits used to exert their influence in the lives of people (1 Cor. 10:20-21).[34] When Jesus quoted Deuteronomy 6:13, He was saying that He would not bow to Satan in the guise of other gods. There could be no substitute for worship, faith and service given to the Lord God, the Creator and rightful Ruler of the universe.[35]

When Jesus was sent by the Spirit into the wilderness to do battle with Satan, Jesus struggled against Satan by speaking God's Word. These words were the Spirit's sword (Eph. 6:17; Heb. 4:12) which God used to defeat Satan. One reason these words had authority over Satan was that they were spoken by the Son of God. As the incarnate Son of God, Jesus has God's absolute authority over heaven and earth (Matt. 28:18). This includes authority over all the spiritual powers in the universe, including Satan. During Jesus' earthly ministry there were many times when He commanded evil spirits to leave people. Because of Jesus' unique authority as the Son of God, these spirits had no choice but to obey Him (Matt. 8:29; Mark 5:7; Luke 8:28).

Jesus' words also had power because they were from the Scriptures. At this point we must be very careful. While the words of the

Bible do have power, this is not power in a magical sense. We must not think of the words of the Bible as incantations which, when recited, will always bring about the results we desire. There are many examples in Christian history, beginning with the book of Acts, of people who tried to exert spiritual power through the use of specific Christian words and actions. Simon the Samaritan sorcerer thought he could purchase the power of the Holy Spirit (Acts 8:18-19). And the seven sons of Sceva, a Jewish priest in Ephesus, tried unsuccessfully to drive out evil spirits using the name of Jesus (Acts 19:13-16).

Timothy Warner warns against the view that "saying the right words" or even using the name of Jesus guarantee that we will be able to defeat Satan. "Effectiveness" in our struggle against Satan, Warner writes, depends of the degree that a person is "living and serving under the authority of the Lord Jesus Christ."[36]

Jesus did not quote Deuteronomy with the expectation that merely the use of the Scriptures would cause Satan to flee. When Jesus spoke God's Word there was power because Jesus *embodied* the truth of this Word in His own life. Jesus not only spoke God's Word; in Jesus the "Word became flesh and made his dwelling among us" (John 1:1, 14). Jesus fleshed out the truth of God's Word. Jesus' work on earth, beginning with His miraculous birth and culminating in the cross and resurrection, was God acting through the "humanness of Jesus" to do "what only God can do."[37] As a result, when people meet Jesus, they meet the one and only true God. Jesus spoke with complete honesty when He said, "I am the truth," and "If you really knew me, you would know my Father as well" (John 14:6, 7).

The most overwhelming aspect of this truth found in Jesus Christ is God's love for the whole world (John 3:16) which resulted in sending His Son to be the atoning sacrifice for our sins (1 John 2:2; 4:9-10). God entered the "world of sin and death in order to overcome sin and death by making atonement for sin on the cross and by breaking the power of death through rising from the dead and ascending into heaven."[38] In Christ, God shows that His purpose for creation was not altered when Satan fell and took the world with Him. Although the world in which we live remains flawed by the curse of sin, God has paid for its redemption through His Son, Jesus.[39] This is why the heart of Christian mission is helping people "realize that truth can be known, and truth *is* known in the person of Jesus Christ."[40]

My wife and I were meeting with another couple for worship and Bible study. The husband was a new believer, but his wife was still seeking the truth. The wife asked me, "What does it mean to pray in Jesus' name?" Those of us who have been Christians for many years pray in Jesus' name habitually, sometimes almost unconsciously mouthing the words without thinking about their significance. But I realized at the moment I heard this woman's question that the issue she was raising penetrated to the very heart of what it means to be a Christian. The truth that is found in Christ makes a difference in what we know about God and how we know Him.

I explained that a Christian has a personal relationship with God through faith in Jesus Christ. When we pray in Jesus' name, we are praying through Jesus to God. While people in other religions must have a priest to serve as a spiritual mediator, this is not necessary for the Christian. Through Jesus, we have direct access to God, can know God personally, and can experience God's love and power in our lives.

At this point, the woman's husband shared a word of personal testimony: "I grew up in a Buddhist family. We always had to depend upon the priest in religious matters. But now that I am a Christian, I do not have to do this anymore. I can pray directly to God." This man had met Jesus and had been set free through the power of God's truth. Now he encouraged his wife who has seen Christ's liberating power in her husband's life and yearned for the same experience.

Not only were these words of testimony in response to a woman seeking Christ. They were good news that God came into the world seeking[41] her and many others in need of hope and new life. Those who find Christ find the truth that frees them from sin and death. They experience knowing the one true God who created them and loves them.

Understanding and Applying God's Word

1. ***Why do people reject Jesus Christ?***
2. ***How did the world fall under Satan's influence?***
3. ***What does Satan want to accomplish through His influence in the world?***

4. ***How does Jesus respond to the world's rejection?***
5. ***What is the role of God's Word in overcoming Satan?***
6. ***What are the implications of this understanding of God's Word for your spiritual life?***
7. ***What are the implications for bringing transformation to our world?***

CHAPTER TWO

THE IMPORTANCE OF TRUSTING IN CHRIST

We live in a world where truth is contested. Douglas Groothius writes, "The very idea of absolute, objective and universal truth is considered implausible, held in open contempt or not even seriously considered."[1] Social forces, such as the media, education and public opinion, condition people to believe that truth is relative and that any claim of absolute truth is a danger to human freedom.[2] In many ways, the world has come to resemble the "pre-Christian" world of the first century. While Christians believe in one God, most of the people we interact with don't—they have a "designer faith" in which they worship a "personalized combination" of many gods.[3] The human heart longs for significance, and failing to find it in the merely material, creates idols in an attempt to give spiritual meaning to the world in which we live.[4] Paul writes, "They exchanged the truth of God for a lie, and worshiped and served created things rather than the Creator" (Rom. 1:25).

Even when propositional truth is denied, God's Word has power to bring faith and new life. This is because the core of biblical truth is *personal.* God's Word comes to us in the *person* of Jesus Christ. Jesus meets us and calls upon us to *trust in Him,* placing our lives and eternities in His hands. When people trust in Christ transformation occurs.

Uganda was bitterly divided by civil war during the 1960's. During that horrendous period in their nation's history, thousands of Ugandans turned to faith in Christ. When one pastor was asked why so many conversions had occurred, he responded that people noticed how well "Christian men treated their wives and were attracted to a religion that made such an obvious and important difference."[5] Preaching in Uganda at that time focused on Jesus' death as the means of "forgiveness from sin" and "reconciliation between warring parties." People were convinced of this truth when they *saw* the gospel's power to bring "forgiveness and reconciliation" lived out in a "new form of relationship between husbands and wives."[6] The change in these Christians' hearts effected how they lived. These Ugandan believers were able to love and forgive one another because they had experienced Christ's love and forgiveness. Their families and friends who saw their changed lives were drawn to commit their lives to Christ as well.

When a person believes in Jesus Christ as his or her Lord and Savior what takes place is far more than the affirmation of doctrine. Faith in Christ results in fellowship with the true and living God. The Holy Spirit brings spiritual life.[7] The person is freed from the yoke of sin. As the psalmist writes,

> He does not treat us as our sins deserve or repay us according to our iniquities. For as high as the heavens are above the earth, so great is his love for those who fear him; as far as the east is from the west, so far has he removed our transgressions from us (Ps. 103:10-12).

The effectiveness of evangelism should be measured by changed lives rather than by the number of decisions or baptisms. In many cases there is a significant difference between the number of people who make a "decision" for Christ and the number who are actually baptized. Then there is another large gap between the number of those who receive baptism and those who actually become involved in a local church. Many who make a salvation decision and are baptized never become true followers of Jesus Christ. Effective evangelism only has taken place when the decision to trust in Christ "results in continual following and God-produced fruit." This is because true evangelism is part of the process of making "obedient" and "faithful" followers of Jesus Christ.[8] This relationship with Christ becomes the "prism" through which people view "all of their personal and collective relationships," and results in the transformation of their "life values, allegiances and preoccupations."[9] When faithful disciples live in a way that confirms the gospel's transforming power, their lives proclaim God's Word in a world in search of the truth.

Following Jesus

The Gospels include many examples of those who followed Christ because they trusted in Him. As Jesus walked beside the Sea of Galilee He met Simon and Andrew. Jesus said to them, "Come, follow me and I will make you fishers of men" (Matt. 4:19; Mark 1:17). Later, Jesus employed Simon Peter's boat to speak to a large crowd that had gathered to hear Jesus on the shores of Galilee. After Jesus finished His talk, He said to Simon, "Put out into the deep water, and let down the nets for a catch" (Luke 5:4). As a result of the large number of fish that were caught, Simon realized again that this One standing in his boat was no ordinary man. "Go away from me, Lord," Simon said, "I am sinful man" (Luke 5:8). But Jesus said to Simon, James and John, "Don't be afraid; from now on you will catch men!" These fishermen left everything attached to their former way of life and began a new life as followers of Jesus Christ (Luke 5:10, 11).

Since there are two stories of Jesus calling the fishermen, we can ascertain that their commitment to follow Jesus was not instantaneous. Hesitation caused them to return to their old way of life so that Jesus had to call them again. Jesus found the disciples fishing again even after His resurrection (John 20:1-6). It seems that in times of fear and uncertainty the disciples returned to their old familiar way of life. If Jesus had given up on the disciples the first time they failed to follow through on their commitment, Simon Peter would have been fishing on the Day of Pentecost. Each time the fishermen faltered, Jesus confronted them personally and called them once again to be His disciples—to follow Jesus and do His will based on their *trust* in Him.

Matthew was going about his work as a tax collector when Jesus said, "Follow me." Matthew suddenly left everything and followed Jesus (Matt. 9:9; Luke 5:27-28). The other tax collectors and those waiting in line at the tax tables must have been perplexed when Matthew left behind coins, scales, money bags and tax records to follow Jesus. Before Matthew had relied on money as his means of livelihood, but now he *entrusted* his everyday needs to the One the disciples called, "Lord." Jesus' calling of Matthew reminds us that the "Lord often chooses the most despicable people of this world, redeems them, gives them new hearts, and uses them in remarkable ways."[10]

Matthew threw a banquet for the tax collectors and sinners he had collaborated with on a daily basis. Matthew wanted his friends to meet Jesus! While Jewish religious leaders condemned Jesus for keeping company with these men, Jesus responded that these were the people He came to serve. Jesus came to provide God's healing, mercy and forgiveness for sinners (Matt. 9:10-13; Luke 5:29-32). Matthew's willingness to leave everything in order to follow Christ and his desire to introduce his friends and co-workers to Jesus indicate the high level of *trust* that he placed in the Lord.

Many who gathered to hear Jesus' bread of life discourse (John 6:25-66) did not accept Jesus' teaching that they must "eat His flesh" and "drink His blood" in order to have eternal life (John 6:53, 54). At this point they "turned back and no longer followed him" (John

6:66). When others turned away, the Twelve *trusted* Jesus' words and continued to follow Him (John 6:68-69).

When Jesus arrived in Bethany shortly after Lazarus' death, Martha scolded Him for not arriving sooner, "Lord, if you had been here, my brother would not have died" (John 11:21). Martha expressed both her grief at the loss of her brother and her disappointment at Jesus for not being there to heal Lazarus. These words expressed the agony of an untimely death. Anyone who has ever prayed for a sick family member or friend only to see him pass from this life into eternity knows exactly how Martha felt. But Martha's despair never gave way to hopelessness. Even in the valley of death's shadow, Martha had a deep abiding *trust* in Jesus. Based on this rock solid faith in Christ, she said, "I know that even now God will give you whatever you ask" (John 11:22).

The boundaries of Martha's faith in Christ went far beyond where most of us are willing to tread. We may believe that Jesus is the Great Physician who is able to heal any sickness, but when death comes we have reached our limit. We may say, "Jesus has the power to heal, but in this case He chose not to heal. We have to trust that this was God's best." It does lie within God's power to heal, but God does not always choose to heal, in spite of what we may pray, hope and believe. Martha continued to *trust* in Jesus even after her brother's body in the grave had grown cold.

Jesus weeps with us over the sorrow of a loved one who has passed from this world (John 11:35). But He does so with the eternal perspective of the One who knows what is on the other side of the grave. Jesus said, "I am the resurrection and the life. He who believes in me will live, even though he dies; and whoever lives and believes in me will never die" (John 11:25-26).

While physical death may separate a person from us, it does not separate a person from God. Where a person stands in relationship with Christ depends upon her spiritual rather than her physical condition. Whether physically alive or dead, spiritually a person who believes in Christ is "with the Lord" (2 Cor. 5:6-8). A person who *trusts* in Christ in the present world remains in the Lord's hands forever.

Thomas did not believe that the crucified Jesus had returned to life until he encountered Him face to face. Jesus invited Thomas to place his finger into the nail-scarred hands and to put his hand into the Lord's side (John 20:27). There is no record that Thomas ever did so. Apparently, it was enough for Thomas to *see Jesus*. Thomas fell on his knees at the Lord's feet and worshiped Him saying, "My Lord and my God" (John 20:28). He had turned from doubt to *trust* in Christ.

The one we call "doubting Thomas" went on to become a great evangelist energized by his faith in Christ. There is a strong tradition that Thomas carried the gospel as far as India before being run through by a spear. A number of churches in south India trace their roots to Thomas' ministry in that area in the first century.[11] According to J. Herbert Kane,

> Thomas is reputed to have made thousands of converts during his missionary career. In later years their numbers were greatly reduced by persecution. The

> Christian faith, however, never died out in south India.[12]

The objective of evangelism is not to convince people to believe what we say about Jesus. The objective of evangelism is to encourage people to *trust in Jesus*. There is an important difference. A person may believe everything we say about Jesus—that He was born of a virgin, lived a sinless life, worked many miracles, died on the cross and was resurrected from the dead. The person may even believe that Jesus is God's Son, the Savior of the world, but never really trust in Christ for his or her own salvation. Until a person entrusts his or her life and eternity to Jesus' care, salvation does not take place.

Jesus spoke of this *trust* in terms of *abiding in Him*. The person who trusts in Christ lives in continual fellowship with Him. Those who "remain" in Christ bear fruit, bring glory to God the Father, and show themselves to be Jesus' disciples (John 15:4, 8). Those who trust in Christ turn from their old way of life and follow Jesus. They stay with Jesus when the crowd turns and walks away. They continue to believe in Jesus when the cold fingers of death bring doubt and fear into their hearts. And they go out into a lost world to proclaim the good news of the risen Christ.

Encouraging people to trust in Jesus requires an investment of time and energy. Although some people trust in Jesus the first time they hear the gospel, more often people experience salvation within the context of relationships with other Christians. Elmer Towns and Ed Stetzer note that people usually become involved in "community" with Christians before they make a commitment to Christ.[13] The typical postmodern person connects with other people in order to experience "authentic relationships." We must learn to "connect" with people in a way that allows us to convey the truth of the gospel through meeting their needs.[14] When people *see* Christ's love for them fleshed out through us they will learn to trust in Him.

This may sound new to evangelical Christians who have been taught to lead people to Christ through direct presentations of the gospel. However, this emphasis on relationships is really at the very core of the gospel itself. Jesus came to earth in order dwell among us as God in the flesh (John 1:14). The Lord told Moses, "You cannot see my face, for no one may see my face and live" (Ex. 33:20). Yet in contrast John writes that he had not only "seen," but also "heard" and "touched . . . the Word of life" (1 John 1:1). Jesus spent over thirty years on earth and three intense years in relationship with His apostles so that they could *see* God's Word lived out in the flesh. It is in the context of this relationship that Jesus' followers learned to *trust* in Him.

Elements of Trust in Christ

When sharing the gospel often I am asked how Christianity differs from other religions. For example, Japanese Buddhists pray, follow prescribed rituals, and try to live moral lives. Don't Christians do the same? The best answer I have found for this question is,

"Unlike Buddhism, Christianity is not a religion. Christianity is a personal relationship with God through faith in Jesus Christ." J. Isamu Yamamoto, in reflecting on his own Buddhist background and his decision to become a Christian, writes,

> Although Buddhism and Christianity offer different paths and different summits, they cannot both be true. For if Buddhists hope for nothing beyond the grave, and if Christians are promised eternal life with God beyond the grave, then either one or the other or neither is true. The teachings of Buddha and Jesus Christ cannot both be true. Since my quest has always been to know God as my personal Creator, I cannot accept Buddhism. Buddhism offers many wonderful things, but it does not offer eternal life with a personal God who made me as I am, physically and spiritually.[15]

There are four elements that are essential for authentic trust in Jesus Christ: *decision, repentance, abiding,* and *obedience.* We can see all four elements of trust in Yamamoto's relationship with Jesus. First, he made a *decision* to become a Christian, and as a Christian has remained committed to this decision. Second, Yamamoto *repented* of Buddhism when he turned to Christ. In other words, he turned away from his Buddhist family background, upbringing and faith in order to become a follower of Jesus. Third, Yamamoto's faith came out of his experience of Christ's *presence* in the midst of suffering. He writes,

> I have always gone to Christ. I see in him someone who not only knows exactly what I am experiencing but feels what I feel, as well . . . I have always found Christ's hand reaching for me whenever I am suffering, and for me this has been my only solace.[16]

Finally, even when family members and friends opposed his decision, Yamamoto *obeyed* Jesus' command to follow Him.

These are *elements of trust* rather than *steps* because they are not necessarily sequential. A person does not always begin with decision, and then move step by step through repentance, abiding and obedience. There is some moving back and forth between the elements, and sometimes they occur in a different sequence. For example, a person may repent of his or her old way of life before deciding to follow Jesus.

The elements often are present simultaneously. Rather than occurring only once at a particular point in time, *decision, repentance, abiding,* and *obedience* become ongoing expressions of the believer's trust in Christ. There is a daily decision to follow Christ (Luke 9:23), a continual turning from sin (1 John 1:8-9), the ongoing experience of His personal presence (Matt. 28:20), and consistent obedience which enables us to experience Christ's love and joy in our lives (John 15:9-11). Let's look at these elements in detail.

First, *trust in Christ necessitates a personal decision to follow Him.* Jesus said, "If anyone would come after me, he must deny himself and take up his cross daily and follow me" (Luke 9:23). A person must decide to deny self and to bear the cross in order to follow Jesus. Simon Peter, Matthew, Martha and Thomas all made decisions to lay aside their old ways of life to become Jesus' followers. Until they made the decision to trust in Jesus and follow Him nothing changed. Without this decision Simon and John may have spent the rest of their lives fishing. Matthew would have grown old hovering over the tax table. They would have missed out on the excitement of following Jesus.

Many people equate effective evangelism with the communication of knowledge. They think explaining the gospel clearly is all that is needed to lead people to faith in Christ. Knowledge is necessary for faith in Christ. God gave us His Word because He knew that we need to know about Him in order to believe in Him. However, knowledge in itself does not guarantee trust in Christ. People may reject Jesus when they understand who He is. Jesus experienced this rejection firsthand when He told people they must believe in Him in order to have eternal life. When people understood faith in Christ as the way of salvation, many turned and walked away from Him (John 6:40, 66).

A person must make a *decision* to trust in Christ. Some people may make this decision based on relatively little knowledge, after hearing the gospel for the first time. Other people may need to study the Bible for weeks, months, or even years before they are willing to trust in Christ. A close friend who had heard the gospel for twenty years made the decision to trust in Jesus as her Savior just before she died of cancer. Her knowledge of

God's Word made no difference until she decided to apply what she knew. The results of her decision to trust in Christ are eternal: she is with the Lord now because she decided to trust in Him.

Second, *in order to trust in Christ people must repent of their old way of life.* John the Baptist called on people to repent in order to prepare for the coming of the Messiah (Matt. 3:2; Mark 1:4; Luke 3:3). Simon Peter told the crowd gathered on Pentecost, "Repent and be baptized, every one of you, in the name of Jesus Christ for the forgiveness of your sins" (Acts 2:38). Paul writes, "Godly sorrow brings repentance that leads to salvation and brings no regret" (2 Cor. 7:10). Repentance is God's gift rather than a human work. God provides the opportunity for repentance through instruction in His Word (2 Tim. 2:25).

The Greek word *metanoia,* translated "repentance," literally means "to change one's mind." There are two sides of repentance. One side is "regret" of a thought or action, and the other is "conversion" to a new way of thinking, acting, or living.[17] Repentance moves beyond sorrow to a decision to "make a U-turn away from sin" and move in a different direction. As long as a person continues in the same lifestyle characterized by the same thoughts and the same behavior, repentance is incomplete. "Biblical repentance always brings genuine change."[18]

In Japan there are many cases of people who confess faith in Christ but also continue to worship their ancestors. Rather than trusting exclusively in Christ, they attempt to add faith in Christ to their Buddhist faith. Such people confess faith in Christ with their mouths, but continue to harbor trust in their ancestors in their hearts. They have not turned from their old way of life in order to follow Christ. This lack of repentance results in a two-level belief system in which the person has a thin veneer of Christianity, but their beliefs, values, thoughts and actions continue to be shaped largely by Buddhism.

Syncretism occurs when the "beliefs and practices of opposing systems are modified and accommodated to each other in a way that they become essentially one new system."[19] Syncretism is easy to identify when people believe in many gods. In Japan, for example, many people adhere to both Shinto and Buddhism. Shinto deities and rituals are connected with birth and life while Buddhist beliefs and practices are related to death.[20] However, syncretism is equally prevalent in Western societies where polytheism is not commonly recognized. Many Americans who claim to believe in Christ simultaneously divulge an interest in the ancient practices of the occult, astrology, and mysticism as well as the contemporary idolatries of materialism, pleasure, and social advancement. At the heart of syncretism is an "idolatry" of the self: an attempt to manipulate the "spirit world" for personal protection, profit and advancement.[21]

Many people give up following Jesus because they do not completely trust in Christ. They let Jesus have only a portion of their hearts while they also continue to believe in other gods. Jesus will not accept this arrangement. He is either Lord of all, or He is not Lord at all. And when Jesus is not Lord at all, He gives people over to their hearts' desires (Rom. 1:24, 26, 28). The result is continued domination by the spiritual powers which control the present world.

Jesus tells us we must "deny self" in order to follow Him (Luke 9:23). People cannot continue to grasp the present world with one hand while reaching out to Jesus with the other. When they try to do so, the "spirit of this world" (1 Cor. 2:12) will never let them go. People must give up their pursuit of idols in order to follow Christ. They must turn away from every other source of spiritual power and soulish satisfaction and place their trust completely in Jesus Christ. True Christian faith can never be trust in Jesus plus belief in anything else. It must always be faith in Christ only.

Third, *trust in Christ deepens as people abide in Him.* To abide in Christ means to live in intimate relationship with Him. Jesus said that spiritual fruitfulness is dependent on "remaining" in Him (John 15:1-10). In Ephesians 1, Paul emphasizes that "every spiritual blessing" from God comes to us "in Christ": holiness and purity (Eph. 1:4), "adoption" as God's children (Eph. 1:5), "redemption" and "forgiveness of sins" (Eph. 1:7), "wisdom and understanding" (Eph. 1:8), election to fulfill God's purpose (Eph. 1:11), and "hope . . . for the praise of his glory" (Eph. 1:12, 14).

Richard Foster writes that "interaction with God" through Christ brings a person's character in line with "God's personality and action." The person moves toward spiritual maturity to the "degree that his or her life is correctly integrated into and dominated by God's spiritual Kingdom."[22] The spiritual disciplines, such as prayer, fasting, meditation, and Bible study, are "activities of the mind and body purposefully undertaken, to bring our personality and total being into effective cooperation with the divine order."[23]

When a person spends time with Jesus, the relationship with Him grows stronger, and *trust* in Christ becomes deeper. The foundation of the person's life becomes more deeply embedded in the Rock so that he or she is able to better withstand the storms of life (Matt. 7:24-27). The person who is firmly anchored in Christ can withstand every spiritual onslaught, whether temptation, discouragement, danger or even death.

> Who shall separate from the love of Christ? Shall trouble or hardship or persecution or famine or nakedness or danger or sword . . . No, in all these things we are more than conquerors through him who loved us (Rom. 8:35, 37).

Abiding in Christ produces fruitfulness in the Christian life. Waylon Moore writes, "When a Christian is full of Christ, others see him and hear about him and then are spiritually reborn into the kingdom of God."[24] A woman I know spent many years struggling in her Christian life. Then she had the opportunity to enter a training program that emphasized spiritual growth through repentance and faith in Christ. The woman learned to trust in Christ and to walk with Him daily. She was transformed from a weak, struggling Christian into a person who lived her faith and shared the gospel with others. This led to the opportunity to lead her friends to faith in Christ.

Fourth, *trust in Christ results in obedience to God's Word.* When the crowd turned away from Jesus the Twelve continued to follow Him. Peter explained their response, "Lord, to whom shall we go? You have the words of eternal life" (John 6:68). The difference between the crowd that left and the Twelve that remained was *trust.* The crowd did not believe Jesus' words, but the Twelve believed. And since they believed, they were willing to do what Jesus said, even when it meant swimming against the current of public opinion.

People who impact the world for Christ are those who are willing to obey Christ regardless of the cost. They do not allow the opinions of others to prevent them from doing what Jesus says. Like Peter and John, they say, "It is [not] right in God's sight to obey you rather than God" (Acts 4:19).

William Carey's willingness to obey the Great Commission when others said no enabled him to impact the world for Christ. In 1792, Carey came to the conviction that the Great Commission was intended for all Christians of every generation. He appealed to a group of fellow Baptist ministers for their support in carrying the gospel to the people of other nations. One of the older pastors responded, "Young man, sit down. When God pleases to convert the heathen, He will do so without your aid or mine." Preferring to obey God rather than men, Carey published his famous book, *An Enquiry into the Obligation of Christians to Use Means for the Conversion of the Heathens.* After the publication of his book, Carey had the opportunity to speak to another gathering of ministers in which he said: "Expect great things from God; attempt great things for God." Finally, Carey acted on his faith when he set sail for India in the summer of 1793. During more than forty years of missionary work in India, Carey left his mark through evangelism, church planting, Bible translation and education.[25]

In light of the four elements described here, *trust in Christ* may be summarized as *the decision to turn from sin in order to walk with Christ.* This statement begins with the aspect of *decision,* which brings about *repentance* of the former way of life in order to walk with Christ. This walk with Christ includes both *abiding* in relationship with Him and *obedience* to His commands. Trust in Christ is just as essential for the mature Christian as it is the new convert. It is the primary characteristic of the Christian life, beginning with conversion, continuing in our daily walk with the Lord during the present life, and reaching its culmination in eternity with Him. As Paul writes, we are "with the Lord" (2 Cor. 5:8), whether in this world or the next. It is our Lord's presence with us (Matt. 28:20) that brings God's Word to fruition through us.

Confessing Jesus: The Foundation and the Keys

"Who do *you* say that I am?" With this question, Jesus raised the importance of His identity above human opinion. It was not enough for Jesus' disciples to answer the question, "Who do *people* say that I am?" Each person has to wrestle with the issue of who Jesus is (Matt. 16:13-15).

Who Jesus is and why He came is the heart of God's Word to a world lost in sin. Mark Heim has written that in Christ's life, death and resurrection, the "power of sin and death are overcome with forgiveness and life." Christ is the "decisive self-revelation of God" who "meets the ultimate human need for meaning and truth."[26] In Christ, God has done everything necessary for human beings to know Him and to experience His love and power in their lives. He has defeated Satan, overcome sin, and brought deliverance from evil. Through Jesus Christ, God has provided the opportunity for every person to have an eternal relationship with Him.

Our reception of God's gifts of forgiveness and eternal life depends on our response to Jesus' question, "Who do *you* say that I am?" Simon answered correctly, "You are the Christ, the Son of the living God" (Matt. 16:16). This statement of faith was not only Simon's opinion based on his personal experience with Jesus. It was a conviction that resulted from a supernatural process, brought about by the inner working of God's Spirit. Jesus said, "Blessed are you, Simon son of Jonah, for this was not revealed to you by man, but by my Father in heaven" (Matt. 16:17).

The most obstinate people, who stubbornly resist the gospel for years, may suddenly repent in tears and turn to faith in Christ. The proclamation of the gospel and the prayers of God's people are factors in these decisions. However, the most important factor is the work of the Holy Spirit. And the resulting faith in Christ is God's blessing.

> "For it is by grace you have been saved, through faith—and this is not from yourselves, it is the gift of God" (Eph. 2:8).

Anytime someone confesses faith in Christ, it is the result of God's work. The Holy Spirit guides people "into all truth" (John 16:13) by bearing witness to the truth of Christ. The Spirit's internal witness acts as God's life-giving breath (John 3:6) upon cold, spiritually dead hearts. This is God's creative activity to produce faith and spiritual life (2 Cor. 5:17). New life that results from faith in Christ is a miracle akin to God's creation of the universe at the beginning of time. God creates something out of nothing, and brings life to the nonliving.

In response to Peter's statement of faith, Jesus made two pronouncements that are pivotal for our understanding of the power of God's Word to change lives. First, Jesus said, "You are Peter, and on this rock I will build my church, and the gates of Hades will not overcome it" (Matt. 16:18). While Roman Catholic interpretation of this verse sees Peter as the foundation of the church, many Protestant interpreters see Peter's faith in Christ as the rock. However, the best understanding is that *Jesus Himself is the foundation upon which the church must be built.*

This interpretation is consistent with Jesus' parable of the wise and foolish builders (Matt. 7:24-27), as well as His claim, "the stone the builders rejected has become the capstone" (Ps. 118:22; Matt. 21:42;

Mark 12:10; Luke 20:17). Paul writes that Jesus Christ is "foundation . . . already laid" (1 Cor. 3:11). Elsewhere, "Christ Jesus himself" is the "chief cornerstone" on which the church is built (Eph. 2:20). Finally, Peter writes that Jesus is the "chosen and precious cornerstone" upon which God's "spiritual house" is being built (1 Pet. 2:4-8). Since the church is founded upon Christ, its foundation is secure and its victory is certain. As R. C. H. Lenski writes, "The implication is that hell's gates shall pour out her hosts to assault the church of Christ, but the church shall not be overthrown (Rev. 20:8, 9). What makes her impregnable is her mighty foundation, Christ, the Son of the living God (1 Cor. 15:24b)."[27]

This understanding of Jesus as the foundation of the church has important implications for Christian mission. First, it reminds us that the church is the result of God's initiative and God's work. God founded the church through His work in Christ, and the church continues to grow and develop on the basis of this foundation. We must be very careful about taking credit for "church planting" and "church growth." The church is God's work from first to last, and it is only by God's grace that we are allowed to have a part in what He is doing. The "message of the cross" which we proclaim "is the power of God" for the salvation of those who believe in Christ (1 Cor. 1:18). It is "only God who makes things grow" (1 Cor. 3:8). God is the "expert builder" who is building the church upon the strong foundation of Jesus Christ (1 Cor. 3:10, 11).

Paul writes that Christ is the "head of the body, the church" (Col. 1:18). Christ's position as head of the church relates to His authority as Lord in that He has "supremacy . . . in all things" (Col. 1:18). Christ's rule over the church stems from His unique role as the *source* of the church's life: Christ is the "beginning and firstborn of the dead" (Col. 1:18), "all [God's] fullness dwells in him" (Col. 1:19), and through Christ "all things" are "reconciled" to God (Col. 1:20).

These expressions relate to soteriology as well as ecclesiology. Our participation in salvation through faith in Christ is linked to Christ's headship over the church in such a way that the two are essentially one. When a person receives Jesus as Savior, he or she also receives Him as Lord. And Christ's exercises His authority within His body, the church. A person who comes under the Lordship of Jesus Christ will also be committed to serve Him through the church.

Colossians 1:18-20 suggests a close relationship between individual salvation and corporate Christianity. To be saved is, by definition, to be a part of the body of Christ. Participation in the body of Christ necessitates meaningful commitment to and participation in a local congregation of believers in Jesus Christ. As we shall see, effective discipleship, in which people learn to obey everything Jesus has commanded (Matt. 28:20), leads to faithful participation in a local church. Spiritual maturity, in which a person is committed to Jesus as Lord, comes about in the context of worship, ministry, and fellowship as a member of local expression of the body of Christ.

In His second statement, Jesus said, "I will give you the keys of the kingdom of heaven; whatever you bind on earth will be bound in heaven, and whatever you loose on earth will be loosed in heaven" (Matt. 16:19). The "keys of the kingdom" are connected with the authority to bind and loose, to lock and unlock, to close and to open. A better translation of the actual Greek wording here is, "Whatever you bind *will have been bound in heaven,* and whatever you loose *will have been loosed in heaven."* The church's use of "the keys" is predetermined by God's will to bind and to loose.[28]

In Peter's confession of faith we find "the keys of the kingdom of heaven." When our words acknowledge the deity and authority of Jesus Christ, our message bears witness to Christ's power to set people free from spiritual bondage. Whether the hearer experiences this spiritual freedom or continues in bondage to sin and death depends upon his or her response to the gospel.

Notice that Jesus said, "*whatever* is bound or loosed" rather than "*whoever* is bound or loosed" (Matt. 16:19, author's emphasis). Christ's power to free people from sin and death comes to them through the proclamation of the gospel. People (the *whoever)* experience this freedom when the evil spirits that influence their lives (the *whatever)* are bound by the authority of Jesus Christ.[29] When we proclaim the gospel, the hearer is confronted with the truth of God's Word. When the hearer accepts this truth in faith, the power of Satan, the father of lies, is bound. The dragon is chained so that he no longer has free reign to influence every aspect of the person's life. The more that God's Word is understood, accepted as truth, and applied to the person's life, the more limited Satan's influence becomes. It is this power of God's Word to bind Satan and free the believer that Jesus is referring to when He says, "If you hold to my teaching, you are really my disciples. Then you will know the truth, and the truth will set you free" (John 8:31-32).

A new Christian that I know is rapidly growing in her faith. She attributes this spiritual growth to her ravenous hunger for God's Word and her effort to apply it to everyday life. Prior to becoming a Christian, this woman distrusted people because she had endured rejection and ridicule from others. She also suffered due to the disability of one of her children. Since becoming a Christian, these circumstances in her life have not changed. Her child is still disabled and sometimes the woman still is ridiculed and put down. But her life has changed because she has experienced the truth that God loves her and walks with her through every circumstance. She no longer allows Satan to use these difficulties to discourage her. The power of the gospel has freed her from spiritual oppression. Tears of disappointment and sorrow have been replaced by tears of joy.

Walking in the Light

When a missionary taught about Jesus' birth non-Christians participating in the Bible study responded, "Do you expect us to believe that a virgin became pregnant and had a son? And what you said about angels appearing to shepherds on a hillside—how can that be true?"

In our world, faith in an unseen God whose Son walked the earth two thousand years ago often is portrayed as a leap into oblivion. Uncertainty is commended as the greatest good, and living in doubt is considered preferable to putting hope in something that might not be true. The old adage, "Seeing is believing," has been personalized to the maximum degree. How something is *seen* is a matter of personal perspective. What is considered true by one person may be thought of as false by her neighbor. One might say, "If you want to believe that Jesus' mother was a virgin, more power to you. Just don't expect me to join your party."

When we ask people to trust in Christ for their salvation, they may think that we are asking them to step into the shadows of obscurity. On the contrary, we are calling them to step out of the darkness into the light. Jesus came to "shine on those living in darkness and in the shadow of death, to guide our feet into the path of peace" (Luke 1:79).

> God is light; in him there is no darkness at all. . . . If we walk in the light as he is in the light, we have fellowship with one another, and the blood of Jesus, his Son, purifies us from all sin (1 John 1:5, 7).

C. S. Lewis writes that his conversion from atheism to Christianity was a metamorphosis from belief in no god at all to belief in a god, to belief in the God, to faith in the God who was made flesh and revealed Himself to us in Jesus Christ.[30] Coming to faith in Christ is a transformation from the ambiguity of life in the everyday world to the certainty of a relationship with God. In this relationship, the abstract and unknowable is replaced by the concrete and real. It is what has been "seen" and "looked at" and "touched" which is "proclaimed" and believed in as the "Word of life" (1 John 1:1). In a word, Christian faith is trust in Christ. Francis Schaeffer writes,

> True Christian faith rests on content. It is not a vague thing which takes the place of real understanding, nor is it the strength of belief which is of value. *The true basis for faith is not the faith itself, but the work which Christ has finished on the cross.* My believing is not the basis for being saved—the basis is the work of Christ. Christian faith is turned outward to an objective person: "Believe on the Lord Jesus, and thou shalt be saved."[31]

People's fear of trusting in Christ is, in reality, a fear of entrusting their lives to the only One who can bring confidence in the midst of chaos. "Faith is being sure of what we hope for and certain of what we do not see" (Heb. 11:1) has been painted to mean asking people to believe the unbelievable. Believing in the unseen is having faith when evidence is lacking. It is said, "Even when you can't see it, you've just got to believe."

But Hebrews 11:1 really is not about having faith without sight. It is about *having sight as a result of faith.* Faith enables us to *see* what remains invisible to those who have been blinded by the "god of this age" (2 Cor. 4:4). This sight that comes through faith is the clearest vision of all.

For the person without faith in Christ, life in this world is like walking through a dark room. The person continually runs into obstacles, trips and falls because he or she cannot see. When the person believes in Christ, the light is turned on. The true condition in which the person lives becomes clear. He or she is able to avoid the obstacles and pitfalls of this life. It is even possible to discern a clear path to make it safely the other side. This is the meaning of *salvation*. Jesus Christ rescues people from the perils of this life and shows them the way to God who is waiting with open arms to receive them.

In the 1970's and early 1980's, New York City was characterized by violent crime, rioting, burned out buildings, rampant drug abuse, and a growing AIDS epidemic. The situation became so bad that police in East New York wore T-shirts that said "The Killing Fields."[32] In the mid-1980's, however, planting new churches and renewing older churches began to take place in New York. By the late 1990's a new church was being started every three weeks in the South Bronx. According to a recent study by Columbia University, there are now over 7,100 evangelical, charismatic and Pentecostal churches in New York City.[33]

These churches have become points of light in a dark city. Christians in New York have a network to impact their city through such ministries as bookstores, housing construction, food distribution and the arts.

Their vision is to make Christ known in New York "through compassionate service, principled politics, and multicultural arts." A common slogan is, "God's presence is everywhere." Spiritual hope flourishes as Christians shine the light of Christ throughout their city. One woman commented, "The best gift I have ever received is the gift of Jesus."[34]

People who walk in the light of Christ shine His light into a world darkened by sin so that others can find the light as well. Let your "light shine before men, that they may see your good deeds and praise your Father in heaven" (Matt. 5:16). Towns and Stetzer write that our task is to

> take the light into darkness without being consumed by that darkness. . . . It is necessary for us to continually press on toward the very edge of darkness. It is upon that edge where the power of God becomes most evident—bringing those from darkness to the light.[35]

It does little good to press into the darkness if the light we carry is flickering because we have a poor connection with the power source. So often we allow other priorities to take precedence over trust in Christ. We may place more faith in our planning, our ability, and our resources than we do in Christ. Such faith is idolatry, even when it is done in the name of making disciples. We will not complete the task Christ has called us to when we substitute the task for Christ Himself. The light of Christ only shines brightly through us when we trust in Christ and live on the basis of our faith in Him. We must live in a way that clearly portrays a *decision* to follow Christ, *turning* from our former way of life, *abiding* in Christ, and *obedience* to Him. When other people see Christ's light *through our deeds* produced by faith in Him they will glorify God by turning to faith in His Son.

Understanding and Applying God's Word

1. ***How should we measure effectiveness in evangelism?***
2. ***How does trust in Christ bring about change in a person's life?***
3. ***What is the relationship between repentance and faith in Christ?***
4. ***What is syncretism?***
5. ***What is the foundation of the church (Matthew 16:18)?***
6. ***What does it mean for the church to have the "keys of the kingdom" (Matthew 16:19)?***
7. ***What are the implications of the need for trust in Christ for my own spiritual life?***
8. ***What are the implications of trust in Christ for bringing transformation to our world?***

CHAPTER THREE

THE TRANSFORMING POWER OF GOD'S WORD

When I was leading a seminar on personal evangelism in Tokyo, I asked participants to share about how they came to faith in Christ. One young woman talked about her time in high school when she was bullied, ridiculed and rejected by other students. When she came to a point of complete dejection, through the loving concern of Christian family and friends, she found hope and new life through faith in Jesus Christ.

A young man said that during his student days he had no interest in religion. He was only interested in getting a job and establishing himself, independent from his family. He dropped out of high school and moved to Tokyo to begin this new life. Soon after his move he was involved in a severe automobile accident which necessitated many months of rehabilitation. He became depressed and felt he had nothing to live for. At this point, the encouragement and witness of Christian friends caused him to turn to faith in Christ. Reflecting on this experience, the young man said, "At that time, I realized my only possible hope was in Christ, so I turned to Him."

The similarity of these two testimonies points toward a crucial spiritual truth. When people come to the point of dying to self, they are ready to begin new lives as followers of Jesus Christ. New birth into God's family comes through death to the old life. Citizenship in God's kingdom comes through renouncement of the present world.

Radical transformation results when we share God's Word with other people. Determination and consistency in sharing God's Word with others results when we place the highest priority on this responsibility. As Philip Turner writes,

> Christians must assume the gospel narrative is true, that our lives in a most fundamental way depend upon holding to that truth in obedient faith, that the truth made known in Christ is a matter of life and death, that it is a truth worth dying for, and that as a consequence we are constrained both by love of God and love of neighbor to witness to what we hold to be true.[1]

Consider the young man and woman referred to in the opening paragraphs of this chapter. If Christian family and friends had not taken time to reach out to them and share Christ's love in both deed and word, it is likely that both of them would have passed from a helpless life into a hopeless eternity.

Effective communication of the gospel cannot be reduced to only human interaction. No amount of Christian compassion or personal persuasion can bring about faith in Christ unless God is involved as well. When God's Word is shared, a supernatural process takes place in which God is the "transcendent agent" who "acts in the life" of the hearer, making the claims of the future kingdom visible in his or her life in the present.[2] When the gospel is proclaimed, the Author of this Word speaks to the hearer, "illuminating" its truth and bringing life through the power of the Holy Spirit.[3]

The work of God's Word and His Spirit does not end when a person becomes a Christian. The spiritual transformation that begins at conversion continues throughout the Christian life. The Spirit's goal is that we know Christ intimately, experiencing daily the "power of his resurrection" as we share in the "fellowship" of Christ's "suffering" and "death." Only then can we "attain" the fullness of life which He has for us (Phil. 3:10-16).

Defective Discipleship

In their book, *Changing the Mind of Missions: Where Have We Gone Wrong?,* James F. Engel and William A. Dyrness contend that Western Christians often interpret the fulfillment of the Great Commission (Matt. 28:18-20) to mean "communicating a set of biblical propositions to a maximum number of people and declaring them as 'reached' once this takes place."[4] The problem with this view is that it limits "making disciples" to acceptance of biblical truths and participation in Christian activities.

Authentic discipleship "involves a total transformation of the heart and life that impacts not only individuals but families, communities and nations."[5]

There are a number of defective views of discipleship which can prevent us from completing the task of making disciples. Each of these views reduces the demands of the Great Commission. This reductionism comes out of our desire to make Jesus' commands comprehensible for and do-able by the average Christian. We reason that Jesus would never have commanded His people to do the impossible.

The problem with this reduction of the Great Commission is Jesus never intended for people to carry His commands by their own ability. The Great Commission is only *do-able* in light of Jesus' promise, "And surely I am with you always, to the very end of the age" (Matt. 28:20). Jesus intended for His Word to be carried out through the empowering presence of His Holy Spirit.

The first defective view is that discipleship consists only of calling people to faith in Jesus Christ as their Savior. This view is based on such wonderful biblical promises as, "Whoever believes in him (Jesus) shall not perish, but have eternal life" (John 3:16), "believe in the Lord Jesus, and you will be saved" (Acts 16:31), and "Everyone who calls on the name of the Lord will be saved" (Rom. 10:13). Faith in Christ is an essential aspect of discipleship. It is through faith in Christ that a person turns from sin to salvation. However, genuine saving faith is an abiding, growing faith in Christ that enables a person to mature in their relationship to the Master. Far too often the impression is given that the initial momentary act of belief in Jesus is all that is necessary for Christian life. This kind of belief is insufficient to fulfill Jesus' purpose for people to lay everything aside and follow Him (Luke 9:23).

There is a difference between belief that gives up when the going gets tough and faith that causes a person to cling to Christ because the going gets tough (Matt. 13:18-22; John 6:60-68). The writer of Hebrews warns about those "fall away" because they have weak faith (Heb. 5:11-6:6). It is very difficult for those with weak faith who turn away from Christ to repent and come to authentic saving faith later (Heb. 6:4-6). Philip Hughes writes, "The invitation to faith is not an invitation to inactivity but to the perseverance of a pilgrimage, for Christ is not only the source but also the goal of our salvation."[6] Calling people to anything less than the kind of faith that compels them to turn from sin and follow Christ daily results in what Dallas Willard has called the "Great Omission from the Great Commission." Teaching that simple faith suffices allows people to be satisfied with salvation from sin without also calling them to Christ-likeness.[7] In reality, a person who does not trust in Christ enough to follow Him never really experiences the freedom from sin which our Lord intended.

A second defective view sees discipleship accomplished through only participation in Christian meetings: worship gatherings, prayer meetings, Bible study groups, training teams, ministry teams, and fellowship circles. According to this view, the more meetings and the more kinds of meetings people participate in, the more they will grow in their Christian faith. People that only participate in worship will advance to the first stage of development, people that participate regularly in small groups for training, Bible study and prayer will move to the next stage, and people that take part in ministry and missions groups will advance to a higher level of spiritual maturity.

God planned for Christians to be involved corporately with other believers. This mutual interaction between believers takes on some form of group, whether it be two or three gathered in a coffee shop for fellowship and prayer, eight or ten meeting together for Bible study, training or ministry, or a hundred, a thousand or ten thousand massed together to praise God.

Nevertheless, there are some that participate in Bible study and corporate worship for twenty or thirty years but remain only babes in Christ. Gathering together with other believers does not assure that spiritual growth will take place. Ronald Allen and Gordon Borror write, "The real factor in worship is a heart desire for God. The reason it fails to occur in the pew is it fails to occur in daily living."[8] What is true for corporate worship can be said of other Christian gatherings as well. Unless those that gather are responsive to God's Spirit and His Word, participation in meetings will have little affect. Those who come with a heart for God will leave changed. Those whose hearts are sealed off from the working of the Spirit will leave unchanged as if they had never come at all.

A third defective view is that discipleship only is a matter of separation from the present world. The Bible teaches Christians to avoid entanglements with the world. The present world is a place of sin, evil and death under Satan's influence. Jesus said His followers "do not belong to the world" because He has "chosen [us] out of the world" (John 15:19). Troubles, persecution and worries of the present life can prevent God's Word from bearing fruit in a person's life (Matt. 13:21, 22). So we are commanded, "Do not conform any longer to the pattern of this world" (Rom. 12:2), and warned, "Anyone who chooses to be a friend of the world becomes an enemy of God" (James 4:4).

On the other hand, the New Testament warns that human efforts to abstain from evil can lead to legalism if they are not empowered by the Holy Spirit (Gal. 3:3). Mere human effort leads to sin and death (Rom. 6:23; 7:8, 9), but yielding to the control of the Spirit results in freedom from sin and death (Rom. 8:2,9-10). The need is not so much for us to get out of the world as to get the world out of us! And the only way this can happen is yielding to Christ's work in us. The goal of discipleship is not only abstinence from evil. God's intention is for us to be re-created (2 Cor. 5:17) in the likeness of Christ (Eph. 4:13) so that He can carry out His good works through us (Eph. 4:10).

Another defective view is that spiritual growth is only based on knowledge. According to this view, the more one knows about the Bible and God, the more spiritually mature a person becomes. Bible study and theology *are* important. I attended seminary for several years and have a Ph.D. in theology. This was helpful preparation for Christian life and ministry. But biblical and theological training does not result in spiritual maturity unless it is accompanied by a growing personal relationship with Jesus. In fact, sometimes the contrary is true. Knowledge of God without trust in Christ can lead to arrogance and the pursuit of salvation through a person's own abilities.

Early in Christian history, *Gnosticism* developed. This term comes from the Greek word *gnosis,* meaning "knowledge." *Gnosticism* taught that salvation and spiritual growth were the results of possessing special knowledge about spiritual things. However, the *Gnostics* denied the literal humanity, physical death and bodily resurrection of Jesus Christ. Their effort to elevate the spiritual while denigrating the physical was condemned as heresy by the early church.[9]

In today's world, both Jehovah's Witnesses and Mormons have a great deal of Bible knowledge. Yet they are not spiritually mature Christians. In spite of their knowledge, they are lost because they depend on their own efforts rather than trusting in Christ for their salvation.

We often make the same mistake. We encourage people to take sermon notes, to attend Bible studies, and to read biblical and theological books so they will have a thorough understanding of Christianity, but do not call them to trust in Christ and to obey His commands. The gospel "message becomes barren of substance where there is little tangible behavior to substantiate our claims."[10] This brand of discipleship results in knowledgeable, yet prideful spiritually immature Christians who have taken root at the point of their immaturity and refuse to grow. Many people make so little progress in the Christian life that it is difficult to determine whether or not they are really saved. Unless they have a fresh encounter with God's Word and His Spirit, they will not change.

A fifth defective view is that discipleship is accomplished through only behavior modification. One form of the behavior modification view sees *psychotherapy* as the primary means of discipleship. Christian counseling is extremely important because it can help people move away from destructive patterns of behavior. As the harmful affects of relational dysfunction takes it toll on individuals and families, the need for qualified Christian counselors who can administer spiritual, psychological and emotional healing will become even greater. The key to effective Christian counseling is helping people establish a biblically based personal relationship with Jesus Christ that can stand firm during life's storms (Matt. 7:24-25). Neil Anderson writes,

> When your belief system about God and yourself is shaky, your day-to-day behavior will be shaky. But when your belief system is intact and your relationship with God is based on truth, you'll have very little trouble working out the practical aspects of daily Christianity.[11]

However, counseling alone cannot bring about spiritual maturity. In the physical realm, a physician may heal, but proper nutrition, exercise and rest also are needed for the body to become strong. While spiritual and emotional healing is needed, spiritual maturity requires nutrition, exercise and rest as well. Spiritual growth comes about through a steady diet on the "solid food" of God's Word (Heb. 5:12-14), exercise through a daily personal walk with Christ, and regular rejuvenation through times of worship and fellowship with Him.

Another form of the behavior modification view reduces discipleship to *task training*. According to this view, when people are trained to *do* what Christians are supposed to do they will grow as disciples. This is based on Jesus' command to teach people to "obey everything I have commanded you" (Matt. 28:20). Discipleship is accomplished by training people to read their Bibles, pray, witness, serve others and tithe. Regular accountability in mentoring relationships is used to assure the effectiveness of this process. The goal is to train people who will be effective in training others (2 Tim. 2:2) in a continual process of reproducing and multiplying disciples.

This equation of discipleship with task training often results in the kind of legalism addressed by Paul in his letter to the church at Galatia. False teachers had taught the Galatians that people are saved by faith in Christ, but grow spiritually by *obedience* to the law (3:1-4; 4:8-10). The Galatians were obeying "weak and miserable principles" (4:9) which they had derived from the Old Testament.

Biblically based principles had been misused so that the importance of human ability was over-emphasized in place of a vital relationship with Christ. We make the same mistake when we tell people doing the right things will make them "good Christians." In reality, this strategy loads people down with burdens God never intended for them to bear.

The Spirit's work enables us to believe in Christ (Gal. 3:4) and to become God's children (Gal. 4:6). We are justified "through faith in Christ" (Gal. 3:22) rather than by obligatory obedience to any manmade standards or rules, even if they are based on biblical principles. Only the Holy Spirit can free us from the "desires of the sinful nature" (Gal.5:16, 17) and produce the "fruit" of Christ's character in us (Gal. 5:22, 23). Paul concludes, "Since we live by the Spirit, let us keep in step with the Spirit" (Gal. 5:25). The goal of discipleship is transformation into the image of Christ brought about by the work of His Spirit in us.

A sixth defective view sees Christian maturity as the result of spiritual triumphalism. One form of this view could be defined as *discipleship by exorcism.* Those who hold this position emphasize that demonic influence leads to sin, guilt, discouragement, depression, and even death. In order to be freed from evil, people must be set free from bondage to evil spirits. This freedom from spiritual bondage is brought about through exorcism.

It is important to acknowledge the need for and validity of exorcism. As we saw in the first chapter of this book, the Bible teaches there really are evil spirits which exercise "control over everyday life and eternal destiny."[12] These spirits may have considerable influence over people, communities and even nations. Jesus not only believed in evil spirits. He also confronted them and exorcised them (Matt. 4:24; 8:16; Mark 3:22; 9:25-26; Luke 4:41). The book of Acts also shows the early disciples often involved in the ministry of exorcism (5:16; 8:7; 16:16-18; 19:12).

As we carry out Christ's command to disciple the nations, we should expect Satan and his demonic cohort to give ground very begrudgingly. There may be times when we are called upon to command evil spirits to leave persons in the name of Christ. Then, like the seventy-two appointed by the Lord, we will able to say with great joy, "Lord, even the demons submit to us in your name" (Luke 10:17).

However, when a person is freed from demonic influence without being filled by the Holy Spirit, his or her heart is like an empty room in need of a tenant. We can be certain that evil spirits will not allow such prime real estate to remain unoccupied for long. Jesus said,

> "When an evil spirit comes out of a man, it goes through arid places seeking rest and does not find it. Then it says, 'I will return to the house that I left.' When it arrives, it finds the house *unoccupied,* swept clean and put in order. Then it goes and takes with it seven other spirits more wicked than itself, and they go in and live there. And the final condition of that man is worse than the first. That is how it will be for this wicked generation"

(Matt. 12:43-45, emphasis mine).

The only way to prevent this sorry state of affairs is to be certain that when evil spirits come knocking, God's Spirit is there to answer, "This house is mine, and it is not for sale." When the Holy Spirit is allowed to take full possession of a person's spirit, soul and body, He does not allow room for evil spirits to operate. And God's Spirit recreates the person (2 Cor. 5:17) in the image of Christ. Paul emphasizes this point when he writes,

> Do you not know that your body is a temple of the Holy Spirit, who is in you, whom you have received from God? You are not your own; you were bought with a price. Therefore honor God with your body (1 Cor. 6:19-20).

The key to both spiritual freedom and spiritual maturity is allowing the Holy Spirit to appropriate the "resources" which God has made available to believers through "union with Christ."[13] When we do this, the same authority which Christ exercised over evil spirits during His earthly ministry is made available in us through the Holy Spirit.

The proclamation of the gospel provides the opportunity for the Spirit's work. John Dawson writes, "The gospel must transform the spiritual, philosophical, and physical life."[14] Jesus did not pay the price for our sins on the cross (Rom. 5:8) so that we could become spiritual free agents, doing whatever we want in this world. Rather, through this spiritual transaction we have become God's possessions.

God is our rightful owner through creation, and He acts to take possession of His property through redemption.

Another form of spiritual triumphalism suggests that *spiritual perfection is the result of spirit-filled worship.* This view is more concerned about the external aspects than the internal qualities of worship. Discussions of worship tend to focus on the style of music (either traditional or contemporary), the use of Scripture (either liturgical or basic Scripture reading), the sermon (either too long or too pop-culture), and the order (the placement of offering, communion, prayers, etc.). If all of the elements of worship are right, people will be moved into God's presence, and this "experience of the divine" will be life-changing.

The problem is that many people who rejoice in God's presence on Sunday live like the devil the other six days of the week. Worship has become a "spectator experience" rather than an expression of authentic relationship with God.[15] This is true whether worship takes place in pipe-organ filled, thousand voice choir cathedrals, hand-raising rafter-swinging charismatic congregations, or anywhere on the continuum in between.

"Genuine experiences with the living God" are characterized by a sense of "God's nearness" which fosters a sense of spiritual oneness with other believers and transforms them to become more like Christ.[16] This kind of transformation only takes place when worship "attributes worthship to God."[17] We must focus our attention on God, give Him the honor He is due, and allow Him the opportunity to change us. God is not seeking happy people who have a deep sense of personal fulfillment. "God is seeking worshipers . . . from every tribe and every corner of the earth"[18] who will worship Him "in Spirit and truth" (John 4:23).

The Double-Edged Sword

The proclamation of God's Word in the power of the Spirit brings life. Hebrews 4:12 tells us the "word of God is living and active." God has given this Word to us.[19] Until the time of the Reformation, the "Word" in this passage was understood to refer to Jesus Christ. Many scholars now reject this early Christological understanding, preferring to see the Word as Scripture or the proclaimed Word of God. The argument for this change of interpretation is the lack of an explicit reference to Christ in the immediate context.[20]

On the other hand, Hebrews 4:12-13 occurs in the broader context of one of the greatest Christological treatises in the New Testament. The writer of Hebrews begins by telling us God "has *spoken* to us *by his Son*" (1:2, emphases mine). Christ is the Word through whom God has spoken to us. God's revelation in Christ is the "exact representation" of His glory and the means by which God sustains His creation (Heb. 1:3). Christ is so "superior" to the angels in heaven (Heb. 1:4), that they both "worship him" (Heb. 1:6) and submit to Christ's authority as "ministering spirits" (Heb. 1:14). While "everything was subject to him" (Heb. 2:8), Jesus lowered Himself and "suffered death . . . for everyone" (Heb. 2:9). In doing so, Jesus made "atonement for the sins" (Heb. 2:18) of all who place their faith in Him. The reader is directed to "fix your thoughts on Jesus, the apostle and high priest whom we confess" (Heb. 3:1). Jesus is the great "high priest" who provides us with "mercy and . . . grace to help us in our time of need" (Heb. 4:15, 16). "He became the source of eternal salvation for all who obey him" (Heb. 5:9). "By one sacrifice He has made perfect forever those who are being made holy" (Heb. 10:14).

The "Word" which comes from God is the good news of Jesus Christ. The gospel is not only a message about Christ. Through the "Spirit of Christ" (Rom. 8:9-10; Eph. 3:16-17), *Jesus Himself meets us in the proclamation of His Word, coaxing us to believe in Him.* William Manson writes that it is "God's Word to us in Christ" that enables us to participate in eternal life. As "partakers in Christ" we follow Him "into the life of the world to come."[21] This faith in the gospel is, then, a personal trust in Christ which enables the believer to enter into God's rest (Heb. 4:2-3).

In Revelation 19, the "Word of God," described as a warrior riding on a white horse, is called "Faithful and True" (Rev. 19:11). This Word is not a spoken or written message, but is enfleshed as a living, active person who is none other than the Lord Jesus Christ. Jesus battles against those who are unfaithful, unreliable and false. God's Word is clothed in a "robe dipped in blood" (Rev. 19:13).

The ultimate revelation of God's truth is not found in theological doctrine, religious ritual or ethical behavior. It is found in God's Son nailed to a Roman cross clothed only in His own blood. While this image is grotesque to the human imagination, it reveals both God's power and His love. God's power at work through the cross of Christ frees people from sin and evil and gives them eternal life.[22] And God's love revealed through the death of His Son (1 John 4:9-10) compels us to believe in Him (John 3:16).

The "armies of heaven" that follow God's Word into battle are "dressed in fine linen, white and clean" (Rev. 19:14). Their clothing is identical to that of the "Bride of Christ" (Rev. 19:8). These are the "victorious saints"[23] whose stains have been washed away by the blood of the Lamb (Isa. 1:18; John 1:29). Now clothed in the "righteousness of Christ," their lives bear testimony to the "truth" of Jesus (Rev. 19:9, 10). Here we see the connection between God's revelation in Christ and the testimonies of Christ's followers who bear witness for Him. The testimony of the saints must not be limited to the words they speak on Christ's behalf. For these words to have any power, their testimonies must include the witness of lives cleansed from sin by the blood of Christ.

I talked with a young woman who had only been a Christian for six months. She attended a Christian college in Japan where she learned about Christianity from committed Christian professors. Then she went to the United States for graduate study where she was "adopted" by a Christian family. This family frequently invited the woman to attend church with them at their conservative evangelical church. During this period, she heard the gospel many times, but it remained meaningless to her.

The gospel came to life for this Japanese woman when she was invited to attend a Christian student meeting. At this gathering she was befriended by students that she knew from classes on her campus. The woman began to hang out with these new friends all the time--before class and after class, in the evenings, and on the weekends. Through their life together, the young woman experienced the difference a personal relationship with Jesus Christ made in the lives of her friends. It was this *experience of the gospel* lived out by 20-something-year-old saints that caused this Japanese student living in America to entrust her heart, soul and eternity to Jesus.

God's Word is "living and active" (Heb. 4:12). The Word is "living" because it comes from God who is the source of life and because it has the ability to produce life in those who receive it. Those who receive Christ into their own lives receive with Him the gift of eternal life (John 3:16; Rom. 6:23). "Through Christ Jesus, the Spirit of life" brings freedom from "sin and death" (Rom. 8:2). The Spirit of the one who raised Jesus from the dead "will also give life" to those who have faith in Christ (Rom. 8:11). There is, here, a dynamic interaction between God's Word and His Spirit. The Spirit works with the Word to bring about faith in Christ. And then Christ, working through the Spirit, brings about eternal life.

God's Word is "active" in that it is "effective and powerful."[24] It does not wait passively to be received. Rather, it is "always doing *something*"[25] to incite faith and bring new life. God's Word accomplishes this by acting as a "double-edged sword" which "penetrates even to dividing soul and spirit, joints and marrow" (Heb. 4:12). God's Word in Christ has the power to penetrate the innermost part of our beings, to lay open every thought and motive of our hearts before God. "Nothing in all of creation is hidden from God's sight. Everything is uncovered and laid bare before the eyes of him to whom we must give an account" (Heb. 4:13).

When God's Word penetrates a person's heart, He is not satisfied with enabling the person to make an informed decision about religion. And God is not satisfied with moral and ethical reform. He does not want people who merely participate in Christian meetings, believe Christian teachings or do Christian things. God desires to cut out the old, sinful, decaying debris from our lives and to create something completely new in their place (2 Cor. 5:17).

We must be cautious that we not give ourselves and those we work with the impression that all this *newness* comes at once. At the moment a person trusts in Christ for salvation, he or she is reborn as a new person fit for eternal life in the New Heaven and New Earth (Rev. 21:1-4). Yet, as long as we trod through this present world, much that is *old* remains in us as well. We can say with Paul, "Who will rescue me from this body of death? Thanks be to God—through the Lord Jesus Christ" (Rom. 7:24, 25).

When we disciple other people, there is always a sense in which we are being discipled as well. As we pray and study God's Word together, each person participating in the group comes face to face with the Master. Jesus Himself speaks to us through the words of Scripture, penetrating to the very core of our souls, cutting away the ugliness and dross, informing us of the sins we need to turn from, calling us once again to trust in Christ and to obey His Word.

In order to grasp the power of God's Word, it is important to understand how God's Word brings about a transformed life, and what a transformed life looks like when it comes. Otherwise, we run the race of without the goal in sight. We try to carry out our Lord's command to disciple the nations (Matt. 28:18-20) without clearly understanding discipleship. We think the whole process depends upon us. In reality, it is only God's Word working through the Holy Spirit which has the power to bring about a transformed life.

The Transformation Process

Paul's conversion and subsequent life provide a biblical example of the transformation that occurs as a result of a personal encounter with the living Christ. Prior to his conversion, Saul of Tarsus was considered to be a righteous, religious man. Paul writes concerning his status prior to conversion,

> If anyone else thinks he has reasons to put confidence in the flesh, I have more: circumcised on the eighth day, of the people of Israel, of the tribe of Benjamin, a Hebrew of Hebrews; in regard to the law, a Pharisee; as for zeal, persecuting the church; and for legalistic righteousness, faultless (Phil. 3:4-6).

Saul had been trained by Gamaliel (Acts 22:3), a highly respected and broad-minded teacher of the law. Gamaliel had advised the Sanhedrin to stop persecuting Jesus' disciples. He said, "If their purpose or activity is of human origin, it will fail. But if it is from God, you will not be able to stop these men" (Acts 5:38-39). It seems that Saul had disregarded his teacher's advice. Saul had assented to the stoning of Stephen (Acts 7:58, 8:1). Then he asked the high priest for letters of recommendation to take to the synagogues in Damascus, giving Saul permission to take any Christians he found in that city as prisoners to Jerusalem (Acts 9:1-2).

Saul was on the road nearing Damascus to carry out this threat when he was encountered by the living Christ. He saw a bright light and heard a voice say, "Saul, Saul, why do you persecute me? I am Jesus, whom you are persecuting. Now get up and go into the city, and you will be told what you must do" (Acts 9:4-6). Saul was led blind into the city where he met a man named Annanias, who prayed that Saul's vision would be restored and that he would receive the Holy Spirit. Saul was baptized and then immediately began to "preach in the synagogues that Jesus was the Son of God" (Acts 9:17-20).

As a result of reflection on the change that Jesus brought in his life, Paul writes that he considered everything he once had valued in his old way of life to be "rubbish" which he had thrown aside for the sake of "knowing Christ" (Phil. 3:7-8). He declares that God's Law has value only in so far it enables a person to be aware of his or her sin, but it is incapable of bringing freedom from sin and death (Rom. 7:7-25). Freedom from sin and death only comes through God's gift of His Son, Jesus Christ (Rom. 6:23). It is God's act of grace in sending His Son that results in the salvation of those who have faith in Him (Eph. 2:8). Righteousness comes, not through obedience to the Law, but as God's gift to those who have faith in Christ. So Paul, who was once zealous for the Law, now has as his foremost ambition, "to know Christ and the power of his resurrection and the fellowship of sharing in his sufferings" (Phil. 3:10). His goal is to become like Christ. This is not something he has "already obtained" (Phil. 3:12), but is rather a lifelong ambition for which he continues to "strain" and "press on" (Phil. 3:13, 14).

In Paul's reflection, we find four essential aspects of the transformation process that occurs as a result of an encounter with Jesus Christ, God's living Word. First, there is *recognition of a person's rebellion against God.* Saul had considered himself to be a righteous man who was following the requirements of his religion by persecuting Christians. But then he realized that what he has regarded to be religious activity was really separating him from God.

We often run up against this kind of wall when dealing with people who have other religions and belief systems. They regard their beliefs and practices as the means to righteousness and salvation, and then reject Christ and Christianity based on the opposition of their religion. Religion becomes the means of their rebellion against God rather than the way to God. Adherents of other religions believe they are doing what is right and do not recognize their opposition to God until they come face-to-face with the living Christ.

When Saul met Jesus on the Damascus Road, he came to *understand his need for Christ.* This understanding is the second aspect of the transformation process. Until a person sees her need for Christ, she will not change.

I have seen people participate in Bible studies for years, but still make no commitment to Christ. What holds them back is not a lack of knowledge. They know the essentials of the gospel message so well they can explain it to the average lost person. There actually are cases in which non-Christians have helped other non-Christians to come to faith in Christ, but refused to trust in Christ themselves. What often holds them back is they remain unconvinced of their own need for Jesus.

When people understand the gospel but do not recognize their need for Christ, there are three ways that we can continue to encourage them to turn to Christ: *pray* that the Holy Spirit will convict them of their sin and their need for Christ, *share* Christ's love with them continually through words and actions, and make a *commitment* to give the time, energy and emotion necessary to help them become a growing follower of Jesus Christ. It is not enough to commit to lead them to faith in Christ. Otherwise we will check them off the list at the time of conversion or baptism. We must stick with them until they are pressing forward in their relationship with Christ and their obedience to Him.

The third aspect of the transformation process is that people actually *trust in Christ for salvation.* It was not enough that Saul understood that it was wrong for him to persecute Christians so that he would stop doing it. That only would have changed Saul from a vengeful Jew into a nice Jew. Jesus wanted more than for Saul to stop persecuting His followers. Jesus wanted Saul to follow Him. In order to become an obedient follower of Jesus Christ, Saul had to trust in Him.

This third aspect provides focus to how we proclaim the God's Word. Our goal is to encourage people to trust in Christ. They need to trust in Christ in order to turn away from their old way of life and to receive new life. And they need to trust in Christ in order to grow as obedient disciples. It may come across as overly simplistic, but we cannot say too often, "Believe in Jesus! Trust in Christ!" The Christian life is truly a matter of trust in Him.

When I was in junior high school, I had a Sunday school teacher who, no matter what Scripture we started with, always found a way to bring the lesson to the conclusion, "Life is a matter of believing in Christ." I remember at the time wondering if he was a very good because there was so much repetition. I thought, "Surely, the Bible must be about something else." Over time, I have decided my Sunday school teacher had it right. All of Scripture is intended to encourage us to believe in Christ. That is how we should *teach* the Bible. And if we really want people to catch what we are talking about, that is how we should *live* the Bible as well.

Finally, Paul recognized that *transformation is the result of following Christ.* It is not the result of only a momentary one-time occurrence. And it is not the result of following a set of guidelines that affect only a limited portion of what we do and say. It is an all-encompassing process that affects every aspect of our being, from the moment we say "yes" to Jesus as Lord and Savior until the time when we see Him face-to-face. Knowing Christ and becoming like Him should consume our every thought, emotion and action from dawn to dusk of every day for the rest of our lives. This allows God's Spirit to have free reign to transform our lives through the power of God's Word at work in us.

The Transformed Life

When I was in Tokyo, I worked with the Christian Leadership Training Center (CLTC), which trains local Christian leaders preparing to serve churches and to bear witness for Christ in Japan and around the world. The CLTC curriculum is based on the premise that Christians must grow in three key areas in order to become effective in life and ministry: the *head*, the *heart* and the *hands*. There is a need for *theological* development through *learning* biblical principles, *spiritual* development through *loving* God and other people, and *practical* development for *living* in a way that reflects both biblical principles and love for God and other people.

CLTC's training process is based on a biblical understanding of the task of making disciples. Authentic discipleship comes about through the transformation of the whole person, *head, heart* and *hands,* so that people come to resemble Christ in thought, in spirit and in action. In place of self, people must place Christ at the center of their lives. This involves the ongoing process that Jesus described as "deny self, take up [your] cross daily and follow me" (Luke 9:23).

While becoming like Jesus is a life-long journey, some visible results should show up along the way. First, the transformation process must include a *Christ-centered faith.* Trust in Christ is the initial step in the journey of Christian discipleship. Every subsequent step must be equally based on trust in Christ as well. This is because discipleship is following "in His steps" (1 Pet. 2:21).

The need for Christians to have faith in Christ should be self-evident, but more often than not we get off track somewhere in the discipleship process. We begin by calling people to faith in Christ, but then try to help them advance in the Christian life by developing their commitment to church, to evangelism, to service, to prayer, to Bible study, to missions, or to something else people are to do for Christ and His kingdom. Then people wither spiritually because, like the church at Ephesus, they have "forsaken [their] first love" (Rev. 2:4).

We must remember *whose* disciples we are making! They are to be followers of Jesus Christ. In order for them to learn to walk after Him and to obey Him in every area of life, we must make every effort to keep people connected to Christ, trusting in Him for the needs of both everyday life and eternal life.

This transformation process must also include *Christ-centered living.* Dean Flemming refers to living in accordance with the standards of Christ as "cruciform contextualization": making our "conduct and communication . . . consistent with the gospel in its saving power and Christ-centered content."[26]

I remember during my time as a student missionary in Nagasaki taking a night off to go to a movie. When I returned home, the missionaries I was working with asked me, "How was the movie? Did it point you to Christ? How did it encourage you in your walk with Him?" My initial reaction was, "That's a pretty high standard to have to weigh a movie against." But since that time, I have come to see those questions as the lens through which we should evaluate everything we do. Do the movies we watch, the books we read, and the company we keep point us to Christ? Do our recreation and our work contribute to our growth in Christ-likeness? Few activities are neutral. Almost everything we do will cause us to move either towards Jesus or away from Him. Our thoughts, attitudes, words and actions also will cause others to move either towards Christ or away from Him.

As followers of Jesus Christ, we also must strive to maintain *Christ-centered relationships.* When I teach about Christian marriage, I often draw a triangle. Then I write, "Christ," at the top corner of the triangle, "husband" at one lower corner, and "wife" at the other lower corner. I explain that a Christian marriage is not only a husband-wife relationship; it is a divine-human relationship involving Jesus, the husband and the wife. The primary relational partner for each spouse is Jesus Christ. When Christ is kept in the center of the marriage, the closer each partner draws to Christ, the closer they will draw to one another as well. When both partners are maintaining a close relationship with Jesus, their marriage will thrive.

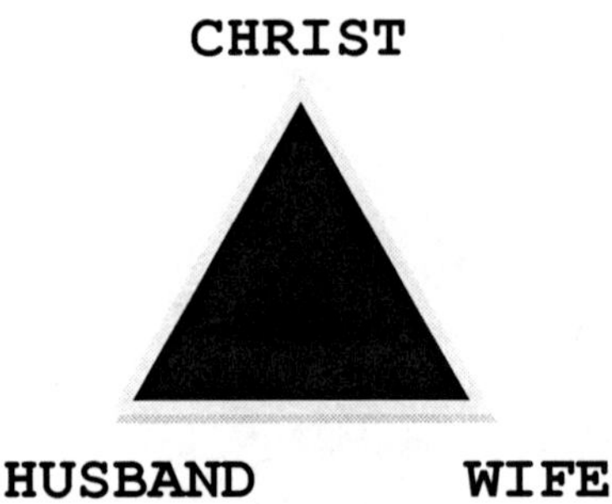

We can apply this same standard to our other relationships as well. When we place Christ in the center of our relationships, and each person draws nearer to Christ, we will experience a closeness and intimacy that otherwise is not possible. The personal presence of Christ as the Holy Spirit becomes the glue which cements our relationships together.

Even in our relationships with non-Christians, in which this kind of Christ-centered fellowship is not possible, Jesus' way of relating to people should become the standard for our interaction with others. This will be characterized by self-giving *love* (John 15:12-13; 1 John 3:16-18), *service* that results in meeting real needs (John 13:1-17), sacrificial *humility* (Phil. 2:5-8), and *forgiveness* for those who have wronged us (Matt. 6:12; Luke 23:34).

When we are making disciples, we may allow something other than Christ to take center in our relationships. Most often this is a task, such as prayer, Bible study, evangelism, or a particular ministry. We focus on encouraging people to carry out tasks and forget about their more basic need: to know Christ and to walk with Him. Even if we succeed in teaching people to carry out tasks, our discipleship becomes ineffective when it is no longer centered on a personal relationship with Jesus Christ.

Another result of a transformed life is the development of a *Christ-centered worldview.* Cultural anthropologists refer to the filters that people use to evaluate truth as their *worldview*. Missionary anthropologist Paul Hiebert defines *worldview* as the "basic categories and assumptions people make about the nature of things and the logic that relates to these to form a coherent understanding of reality."[27] Worldviews include both the questions that people ask about reality and their answers to those questions. Darrow Miller writes,

> The way people and societies answer these questions determines the types of cultures and societies they create. Some answers to these questions lead to poverty and barbarism; others, to development and civilization.[28]

For example, Hinduism teaches that truth is ultimately unknowable and that the material world is an illusion. So those who subscribe to the Hindu worldview may conclude that the pursuit of knowledge and material possessions is a waste of time and energy. This understanding of reality and the way of life that derives from it results in a great deal of the ignorance and poverty we now see in India.[29]

On the other extreme, the naturalist-materialist worldview held by some people in the West dismisses the existence of the supernatural as a "vestigial notion of some less developed stage of man's evolution."[30] Human beings have no spiritual nature with which to commune with the God who created and loves them. As there is no divine spirit, there is no human spirit either. People are "no more than some chance collation of atoms washed ashore on a little planet in a remote corner of a vast cosmos."[31] This view of reality leads to a meaningless notion of existence which results in a sense of purposelessness. Life is taken without much thought: whether through the abortion of an unwanted child, the euthanization of unproductive adult, the annihilation of a meddlesome enemy, or the suicide of a troubled young person. The loss of a sense of the supernatural leads to the death of the natural world.

When a person develops a *Christ-centered worldview*, Jesus Christ becomes the filter through which she evaluates truth. In order for something to be considered true, it must square with what we know of God, the world, human beings, and good and evil, through God's revelation in Christ. When Christ becomes the criterion for determining truth, the claim that there are many gods must be considered false because there is only One God who has revealed Himself to us in Christ. The assertion that there are many possible ways of salvation also is false. Jesus said, "I am the way and the truth and the life. No one comes to the Father except through me" (John 14:6). On the other hand, the belief in the essential worth of human beings is true. God considers us to have such great value that He sent Jesus to provide the necessary means for our redemption. Furthermore, assertions about the reality of evil and the inability of people to overcome evil by ourselves are also true. The Bible teaches God has addressed the problems of evil and suffering personally and finally in the death, resurrection, and final awaited victory of His Son.

The disciple-making process brings about this "shift" in worldview.[32] We should not suppose this takes place instantaneously and completely at the time of conversion to faith in Christ. Actually, the development of a Christian worldview usually begins prior to becoming a Christian when a person accepts the reality of One God who is the Creator and Lord of the universe. Belief in monotheism then leads to the recognition of dependence on this God for one's personal existence. It is in Christ that a person learns about God's love for us and the extreme to which He has gone that He might have a relationship with us. Worldview transformation continues throughout the discipleship process, as the person continues to gain both a broader and a deeper understanding of God who has revealed Himself to us in Christ.

Finally, a transformed life will result in a *Christ-centered purpose.* This consists of laying aside our own wants, desires, plans and dreams in order to live for Christ and His glory. This does not result in the negation of self. Rather, there is a merger of our personal identity with that of Jesus Christ, so that we can say with Paul, "For to me, to live is Christ" (Phil. 1:21). Paul found encouragement in being "united with Christ" (Phil. 2:1) in humility (Phil. 2:5-11) and interest (Phil. 2:21). He was willing to forsake all for the sake of "knowing Christ Jesus" (Phil. 3:7-8), "gaining Christ" (Phil. 3:8), "sharing in his sufferings, becoming like him in his death, and so, somehow, to attain to the resurrection from the dead" (Phil. 3:10-11). This remained a goal for Paul: something he sought for rather than something he had already attained. He continued to "press on to take hold of that for which Christ Jesus took hold of me" (Phil 3:12).

We are called to make disciples who are consumed by their desire to know Christ, to walk with Him, and to experience His transforming power everyday of their lives.

Understanding and Applying God's Word

1. ***What is the fulfillment of the Great Commission?***
2. ***Why do Christians often fail in the process of making disciples?***
3. ***What do all the defective views of discipleship have in common? What do they all leave out?***
4. ***What is the role of God's Word in the disciple-making process?***
5. ***What are some important aspects of a life that has been transformed by Jesus Christ?***
6. ***To what extent has your life been transformed by your relationship with Christ?***
7. ***How can you become more effective in encouraging other people to experience Christ's transforming power in their lives?***

PART TWO

GOD'S WORD IN HIS MISSION

"Go and make disciples of all nations, baptizing them in the name of the Father and of the Son and of the Holy Spirit, and teaching them to obey everything I have commanded you. And surely I am with you always, to the very end of the age." **Matthew 28:19-20**

"Now you are the body of Christ, and each one is a part of it." **1 Corinthians 12:27**

God's mission is to bring people of all nations into a redemptive relationship with Himself through faith in Jesus Christ. Our part in His mission is to live and teach His Word in the power of His Spirit. We carry out God's mission as individuals in personal obedience to the commands of Jesus Christ. We also do so corporately as the Body of Christ, encouraging one another to be God's voice, hands and feet in a fallen world.

CHAPTER FOUR

"GO MAKE DISCIPLES"

In a recent Gallup Poll on Religion conducted in Japan, two-thirds of the respondents said they have no religion. Over half said that they have not heard enough about Christianity to state their impression of it.[1] This relative lack of awareness of Christianity, when coupled with the insular nature of Japanese society, the interest in the occult and other religions, and the mood of "hopelessness" with now pervades the Japanese people, seems to form a "solid, impenetrable wall that could prevent the spread of the Gospel in Japan."[2]

The results of this survey can be reproduced in many countries. In Europe, where official statistics number Christians in the millions,[3] active participation in local churches in some countries is in the range of one to five percent.[4] In Europe and North America, a whole generation has grown up with little or no influence from the Christian faith. Where Christianity once had a prominent place in the public sphere, this has been replaced by a "deeply ingrained prejudice against Christianity" among government policy makers and the general public.[5] Daniele

Hervieu-Leger describes the current situation as the "exculturation of Christianity."[6] Christianity has lost its capacity to influence society because many people have gone through the "process of religious socialization without becoming truly Christian."[7] Carl E. Braaten writes concerning the current situation,

> The Western nations have once again become mission fields, lands populated by neo-pagans, in the grasp of secularism, atheism, and nihilism . . . At the same time millions who would still call themselves Christians are at best nominal church members, ill-grounded in the church's scriptures, creeds, moral teachings, and worship traditions.[8]

The gospel of salvation through faith in Jesus Christ is the most wonderful news in the world. It is this Word from God which is the foundation, heart and thrust of Christian mission. Yet this message is dismissed, devalued, or unknown in our present world. It is *dismissed* by those who refuse to believe in one true God who loves His creation so much that He seeks to redeem it through the atoning gift of His only Son. These rejecters include atheists, pantheists, polytheists, and pluralists. In short, those who see the Christian understanding of truth as too narrow reject Peter's words, "Salvation is found in no one else, for there is no other name under heaven given to men by which we must be saved" (Acts 4:12).

Sadly, the gospel has been *devalued* by many who claim to believe it. It is devalued when it is understood and explained in terms that do not communicate with the lost world. Jesus as Savior is expressed as common knowledge, and scriptures like John 3:16 and 1 John 4:10 are quoted as though everyone both knows and understands them. This conveys the attitude that if people do not believe in Jesus it is their own fault. Certainly, there are many who have heard the gospel and chosen to reject Christ. But it is easy to forget that there are literally billions of people who have never heard the gospel. In our own circle we may know tens or even hundreds of people who have never heard the gospel in a way that makes sense to them. For those who have never heard about Jesus, the gospel is a precious treasure (Matt. 13:44), it is the "words of eternal life" (John 6:68).

For billions of people in today's world, the truth of God's Word remains *unknown*. This includes almost two billion people in hard to reach places in the 10-40 Window[9] who have limited access to a gospel witness. But it also includes tens of millions in places like North America, Western Europe and Japan whose families, friends, education and other influences in their societies have shaped their worldview in such a way that their hearts are closed to God's truth. These people live in places that are geographically open to the gospel, but they live in societies and cultures that are spiritually closed to the gospel. In order for those for whom the gospel remains unknown to have the opportunity to hear and believe, they will need a careful, patient presentation of the gospel that includes both *word* and *deed*. These non-Christians must both *see* and *hear* the gospel's truth before they will be willing to stake their eternal hopes on Jesus Christ. They need to see Christians who have a "passionate love for God and their neighbors"[10] for the gospel message to have any ring of truth for them.

Jesus' command to *make disciples* is usually thought of in relationship to Matthew 28:18-20. However, there are also four other "Great Commission" passages in the New Testament, Mark 16:14-16, Luke 24:45-49, John 20:21-23, and Acts 1:8. These passages do not simply restate the same thing in different ways. Rather, they provide varied emphases which each contribute to understanding our Lord's vision for mission.[11] Jesus sends out His people to proclaim His Word. They are sent out under His authority (Matt. 28:18), to bear witness in the power of the Holy Spirit (Acts 1:8), in order to make the gospel known to the whole world (Mark 16:15). They proclaim God's Word in order to call people to repentance from sin (Luke 24:47) and faith in Jesus Christ (Mark 16:16). Those who accept the gospel and believe will be saved, while those who reject the gospel will be condemned (Mark 16:16; John 20:23). The objective of this proclamation is to *make disciples* among all the peoples of the world (Matt. 28:19). The time frame for the completion of this commission is the end of the age (Matt. 24:13; 28:19-20).

Good News for All Creation

Mark 16:14-16 emphasizes the interaction between faith, proclamation and salvation. When Jesus appeared to the Eleven, first He rebuked them for their lack of faith in the resurrection (Mark 16:14). Since people cannot share what they do not possess, faith in Christ is the most basic requirement for those who bear witness for Christ. Jesus wants to confirm that His followers have the same faith which they ask others to receive. Then Jesus sends them into the world to "preach the good news" so others will believe, be baptized, and be saved.

In the New Testament, authoritative *preaching* about the crucified and resurrected Christ is the normative method by which the gospel is made known.[12] Jesus said, "This gospel of the kingdom will be preached in the whole world . . ." (Matt. 24:14). He sent out the Twelve (Matt. 10:7; Luke 9:2) and then the Seventy-two (Luke 10:9) primarily for the purpose of *preaching*. On the Day of Pentecost the initial act of the church was *preaching* the crucified and resurrected Christ (Acts 2:14-41). When persecution broke out against the church in Jerusalem, the Christians "who had been scattered *preached* the word wherever they went" (Acts 8:4, emphasis added). Paul insisted the people cannot come to faith in Christ unless they hear the gospel *preached* to them (Rom. 10:14). So he instructed Timothy, "*Preach* the Word; be prepared in season and out of season; correct, rebuke and encourage—with great patience and careful instruction" (2 Timothy 4:2).

In the early church, Christians proclaimed the gospel because they believed the message of Jesus Christ truly was *good news* for themselves as well as their hearers. As people heard this message and trusted in Christ, it brought "transformation" to them and, through them, to their society and culture.[13]

Michael Green summarizes the message these Christians proclaimed in three points. First, they preached *the person of Jesus Christ,* centering on the "power and significance" of His cross and resurrection. Second, they preached about *the gift of forgiveness of sin, the Holy Spirit, and reconciliation with God* that comes by God's grace to those who have faith in Christ. Third, *they called for a response.* They called for *repentance from sin* and *faith in Christ.*[14]

The description of *preaching* in the New Testament differs from our contemporary understanding and practice. At the beginning of the twenty-first century, preaching primarily is done by the few for the many. In most churches, preaching is restricted to a few people who have been called and ordained for pastoral ministry. I have a number of books which address the topic of preaching. The perspectives of these books range from traditional to contemporary to emerging church. Almost without exception, these books assume that pastors and others in vocational ministry preach to larger congregations.

This is quite different from the *preaching* described in the New Testament. In Acts 8:1 *all of the Christians* who went out from Jerusalem preached the gospel. Stephen, a layman and deacon by our contemporary understanding (Acts 6:5), was stoned to death for preaching in Jerusalem (Acts 6:8-8:1). The preaching of another deacon (Acts 6:5), Philip, led to revival in Samaria (Acts 8:5-7). Apparently Philip's example carried over to his four daughters "who prophesied" (Acts 21:8), or proclaimed God's Word.

The New Testament does not use the word *preaching* in the restrictive sense of a person standing before a congregation delivering a prepared sermon. Rather, it has the broader meaning of the *verbal proclamation of God's Word*, whether this is done one-on-one, in a small group, or before a large assembly.[15] Green writes that in the early church,

> this must often have not been formal preaching, but the informal chattering to friends and chance acquaintances, in homes and wine shops, on walks, and around market stalls. They went everywhere gossiping the gospel; they did it naturally, enthusiastically, and with the conviction of those who are not paid to say that sort of thing. Consequently, they were taken seriously, and the movement spread.[16]

The purpose of this kind of *preaching* is to extend faith in Christ beyond those who already are His disciples to "all creation" (Mark 16:15).[17] The meaning here is akin to that of "all nations" in Matthew 28:19. Salvation is *inclusive* in that God has provided for the salvation of all the peoples of the world through His Son (Rom. 10:13-17; 1 John 2:2; 2 Pet. 3:9). Mark emphasizes that proclamation of the gospel is necessary because salvation is also *exclusive:* it is limited only to those who believe in Jesus Christ.

This does not allow for the possibility of salvation through other religions. It also eliminates the possibility that all people will be saved through Jesus, whether or not they believe in Him. Finally, it does not allow for the common belief that good, moral people will go to heaven, no matter what they think about God or His Son. Jesus is the only way of salvation for the people of all nations (John 14:6; Acts 4:12), and in order to have this salvation people must believe in Him. In obedience to our Lord's command, "we must become world Christians" who are willing to overcome the barriers of geography, economy, culture and language in order to carry the gospel to the millions of all nations who have never heard.[18]

Today the number of baptisms is counted as though baptism is the distinguishing mark of salvation. Mark 16:16 sometimes is used as a proof text for baptismal regeneration. However, this passage firmly establishes the relationship between faith in Christ and baptism. People are saved through faith in Christ, and baptism takes place afterwards as a "public testimony" of this faith. Water baptism, without faith in Christ, is ineffective to bring about salvation.[19] Baptism is an "outward sign" that a person has entered into a new covenant relationship with Jesus Christ through faith in "His redemptive acts—His death, burial, and resurrection" (Rom. 6:1-4).[20]

On the other hand, *baptism is important* because it professes that, through faith in the Lord Jesus Christ, there has been a break with the past and a new life has begun.[21] The old self has been "crucified" with Christ and the person now lives under the authority of Christ, "freed" from the domination of sin (Rom. 6:6, 7). Baptism is valid only when it is the external expression of the new life brought about internally by the work of the Holy Spirit as a result of person's faith in Christ.[22]

Since baptism confesses to the world the transforming power of God's Word, it is an important *act* of proclamation essential to the church's mission. A few years ago I had the opportunity to baptize a young woman who had just committed her life to Christ. At the close of the service, a man approached me. He had grown up in America, but had never heard the gospel clearly until he moved to Japan for business. Until that day, there had been many things about Christianity he had not understood, but through hearing the young woman's testimony and seeing her baptism, he had come to understand the meaning of salvation. Shortly thereafter, this man committed his life to Christ. Subsequently, he enrolled in a Bible college to prepare for ministry.

On that Sunday morning, I preached a sermon on the nature of baptism and the need for salvation. But it was the "sermon" the young woman preached through her testimony and submission to baptism that wooed this man to faith in Christ. This woman's message had impact because it *showed* what a life entrusted to Christ and transformed by the power of His Spirit looks like. People living in bondage to sin will respond when they see the power of forgiveness wrought by faith in Christ.

God Sends His Love

The heart of Christian theology is the belief that God, because of His love for the world, sent His only Son Jesus Christ to provide forgiveness of sin and eternal life (John 3:16-18). "God is love" (1 John 4:8), and He showed His love when He "sent his Son as an atoning sacrifice for our sins" (1 John 4: 10). God's love for us is not because of our righteousness, but rather is in spite of our sinfulness. "God demonstrates his own love for us in this: While we were still sinners, Christ died for us" (Rom. 5:8).

Missionaries often present a gospel of God's love as the basis for eternal life. But a message only about God's love that makes no mention of human sin is incomprehensible to the lost person. A person who does not understand the depth of his or her sin cannot fathom the expanse of God's love. A person who does not recognize his or her lostness will not grasp the need for the Savior. It was only when Paul realized he was a "wretched" sinner that he was able to acknowledge his need for salvation through Jesus Christ (Rom. 7:23-25). As Paul reflected upon the magnitude of God's gift of salvation he wrote,

> Neither height, nor depth, nor anything else in all creation, will be able to separate us from the *love of God* that is in Christ Jesus our Lord (Rom. 8:39, emphasis added).

John refers to himself as the "disciple whom Jesus loved" (13:23; 20:2; 21:7, 20). John did not think that he was the only one

Jesus loved, or that Jesus loved him more than others, or that Jesus did not love others. John simply recognized the profound truth, "Jesus loves *me*." This awareness that Jesus loved and cherished him compelled John to write, preach and live the gospel in a world marred by enmity and strife.

At the ministry training center where I taught in Tokyo, I asked my students to write a paper on the nature and purpose of Scripture. One student described the Bible as "God's love letter" to us. The Bible tells us about God's love for us, expressed through the gift of His Son, and calls us to love God in response. The Bible calls us to personal relationships with God and other people in which we love God with our total being (Matt. 22:37; Mark 12:30), and love other people sacrificially (John 15:12-13; 1 John 3:16-18), in the same way that we love ourselves (Matt. 22:39; Mark 12:31).

God's love in Christ continues to impact the world through us. Jesus said, "As the Father has sent me, I am sending you" (John 20:21). Jesus' mission did not end when He ascended into heaven (Acts 1:9). Just as Jesus was sent by the Father to do His work (John 5:19-20; 8:29), Jesus sends His followers to continue *Jesus' work*. Just as Jesus spoke the Father's words, Jesus' followers are to speak *Jesus' words.*[23] Just as the Father's love for the world is expressed through sending His Son, even so the Son's love is expressed through His people who He sends out into the world to bear witness for Him.

We will not have any significant impact on the world unless we love as Jesus loved. Timothy George and John Woodbridge remind us,

"There is a direct correlation between the *words* of our message and our daily *walk* before the watching world."[24] People will not believe our message of God's love unless they see His love in us. Jesus said, "All men will know that you are my disciples, if you love one another" (John 13:35). "Love each other as I have loved you. Greater love has no one than this, that he lay down his life for his friends" (John 15:12-13). Francis Schaeffer writes,

> Love . . . is the mark that Christ gave Christians to *wear* before the world. Only with this mark may the world know that Christians are indeed Christians and Jesus was sent by the Father.[25]

The proclamation of the Gospel called for in John 20:19 demands more of us than merely speaking words. Beyond "words" there must also be love "with actions and in truth" (1 John 3:18). This love begins within the Body of Christ. Paul tells his readers, "Love must be sincere . . . Be devoted to one another in brotherly love" (Rom. 12:9, 10). Christians should follow Christ's example by having "compassion" and "forgiveness" for one another (Eph. 4:32). We are to "live a life of love, just as Christ loved us" (Eph. 5:2).

Christ-like love, even within the Body of Christ, is not cheap. A price must be paid so that the world can experience God's love through us. Christians must pay the price of reconciliation and forgiveness. Many non-Christians have told me, "I love Jesus, but I do not love the church. There is too much bickering and fighting there." There is too much truth in these words to dismiss them as only an excuse for rejecting Christ. It is time that we *wage peace* within the Body of Christ. We need to bury our pride and to put too many meaningless feuds that divide God's people to rest. Apology and forgiveness can lead to praying together, worshiping together, witnessing together and working together to share God's Word with a world that needs to experience God's love. Until we are willing to pay this price, many non-Christians will have difficulty recognizing our love, as well as believing in God's love for them in Christ.[26]

Authentic witness for Jesus Christ extends beyond concern for other Christians to love for the world that Jesus came to save. When God's Word becomes embodied in our flesh, it results in meeting the needs of the mind and body as well as the spirit. Jesus said those He knows, that is, those who have a personal relationship with Him, feed the hungry, give drink to the thirsty, provide hospitality for the stranger, clothing for the naked, and encouragement for the sick and prisoners (Matt. 25:37-39). Sacrificial Christ-like love causes Christians to give their own time, energy and material possessions to help those in need (1 John 3:17; Acts 2:44-45; 4:32; James 1:27; 2:14-17).[27]

Rodney Stark, in his book *The Rise of Christianity,* demonstrates that Christian concern for the sick and dying significantly contributed to the growth of Christianity in the second and third centuries. During this time, two major epidemics swept through the Roman Empire, wiping out as much as one-third to one-half of the population. The prevalent response among the general population was fear. With no access to our contemporary understanding of diseases, the ancients tried to avoid illness by isolating themselves. In contrast to the general population, Christians responded with compassion and concern, caring for the needs of the sick and dying. Undoubtedly, some Christian caregivers did become sick and die because of this strategy. But many more Christians than non-Christians survived because their needs were cared for. Over time it became common knowledge that if a person wanted the best chance of survival they should go to the Christians. As a result, a "very substantial number of pagans . . . shifted from mainly pagan to mainly Christian social networks," which led to a substantial number of conversions to faith in Christ.[28]

At the beginning of the 21st century, the threat AIDS is sweeping through vulnerable populations in Africa and Asia. There are over 40 million cases of AIDS worldwide with more than three million deaths each year. A growing number of innocent children have become infected through family members who are HIV positive. We cannot look to governments, NGO's and the United Nations to try to stem the tide. Only Christians, responding with the love of Christ, have the spiritual and moral authority to combat AIDS. This response to AIDS must include medical care for those infected with HIV and AIDS. There should be counseling, food, clothing and other forms of psychological and physical support for those who are widowed and orphaned as a result of AIDS. Biblical teaching on marital fidelity is the most effective means combat the further spread of AIDS. Finally, proclamation of the good news of Jesus Christ will provide eternal hope to individuals, families and nations ravaged by the AIDS crisis.

Jesus sends His followers as ambassadors of love so that the world can experience His peace. Jesus said, "Peace be with you!" (John 20:19, 21). This peace is the result of Jesus' power to overcome turmoil in a troubled world (John 16:33). Through Jesus Christ, the barriers of language, culture, ethnicity and economics which now divide people can be broken down. Moreover, "through faith, we have peace with God through our Lord Jesus Christ" (Rom. 5:1). God has "reconciled us to himself through Christ," and has given us the "ministry of reconciliation" so that, through our proclamation of His message, other people may experience the reconciling power of Jesus Christ as well (2 Cor. 5:18, 19).

This ministry of reconciliation is brought about through *forgiveness.* Jesus said, "If you forgive anyone his sins, they are forgiven; if you do not forgive them, they are not forgiven" (John 20:23). The teachers of the law were correct in their assertion that only God has the power to forgive sins (Mark 2:7). Yet Jesus says that this forgiveness of sin is passed to the world through those whom He has sent. This is because the gospel we proclaim conveys the power of forgiveness. Those who believe our message receive God's gift of forgiveness, while those who reject these words remain bound in their sins.

Forgiveness brings freedom from the old way of life so that people can begin a new life in Christ. Neil Anderson writes that as a result of unforgiveness people are "yoked to their past."[29] Those who are chained in a state of unforgiveness are held in bondage by their sins. These sins prevent them from experiencing the peace and joy which God wills for them. It is forgiveness, made available through Jesus' death on the cross, which has the power to free people from destructive habits and damaged relationships. Forgiveness frees people from guilt and shame. Forgiveness frees people to live as God intended, both now and forever.

There is more to our Lord's commission than preaching the gospel with our words. We must preach the gospel from hearts of love, and live the gospel through acts of service. We must show the world how much Jesus loves them by allowing Him to love them through us. The gospel must be so deeply rooted in us that we embody before the world the rich spiritual blessings which are ours through Jesus Christ: forgiveness, peace, joy and hope. Then the world not only will know we are Jesus' disciples: they will desire to follow Him as well.

Call to Repentance and Forgiveness

Christ's commission to proclaim the gospel to all nations is the continuation of His own mission to provide forgiveness of sins and eternal life for the whole world through His death and resurrection (1 John 2:2). Jesus said that His suffering and death are the basis for the proclamation of "repentance and forgiveness of sins . . . to all nations" (Luke 24:46-47). Early apostolic preaching focused on Jesus' death and resurrection, as well as the need for repentance and forgiveness on the part of the hearers (Acts

2:23-24, 38; 3:19; 4:11-12). Paul writes that salvation results from belief in Jesus' death, burial and resurrection (Rom. 10:9; 1 Cor. 15:1-4; Phil. 3:10-11). Christian preaching, faith and hope all find their basis in the resurrection of Jesus Christ. This connection is so vital that if Jesus did not rise from the dead, our faith has no foundation and we have no hope (1 Cor. 15:14-19). In Revelation, Satan is overcome through both the "blood" of Christ and the "testimony" of those who give their lives for Him (12:11). This witness to the gospel energized by faith in the cross and resurrection of Jesus Christ was the primary reason for the "phenomenal growth" of the early church.[30] Empowered by this faith, within three centuries Christianity grew from a small rabble huddled in an upper room to become the dominant spiritual movement in the Roman world.

In order for the proclamation of Jesus' death and resurrection to bring about change, there must be a response. There must be "repentance" (Luke 24:47). Early Christian preaching called for repentance in response to the work of Christ (Acts 2:38; 3:19; 11:18). Genuine repentance involves a "conscious moral separation, the necessity of forsaking sin and entering into fellowship with God." One of the best known expressions of genuine repentance is 2 Chronicles 7:14: "If my people, who are called by my name, will humble themselves and pray and seek my face and turn from their wicked ways, then I will hear from heaven and will forgive their sin and will heal their land."[31] People cannot experience new life in Christ while also continuing to live as they always have lived. There must be a change of direction. People must *deny self* in order to *follow Jesus* (Luke 9:23). *Sin must be turned from before forgiveness can be received.*

Contrast the response to sin in the lives of Judas and Peter. Both of them betrayed Jesus. Both men stood before Christ as guilty sinners. Both Judas and Peter felt genuine remorse for their actions. Peter experienced new life through "restored fellowship" with Jesus, while Judas' "awareness of sin led only to despair and self-destruction."[32] Judas hung himself while Peter went on to become a dynamic leader in the early church. Why the difference? Both men felt remorse, but only Peter repented. Only Peter turned from his sin and continued to follow Jesus.

When Peter tells the crowd on the Day of Pentecost, "Repent and be baptized, every one of you, in the name of Jesus Christ for the forgiveness of your sins" (Acts 2:38), he not only is preaching a doctrinal sermon based on Jesus' teaching. Peter is preaching spiritual truth based on his personal experience of Christ's redemptive work in his life. Peter knew first-hand the power of God's forgiveness, and he wanted others to experience it as well.

One reason for an absence of power in contemporary preaching is the refusal of preachers to turn from their own sin. Until genuine repentance occurs, sin continues to "dwell" in us (Rom. 7:20). As long as the presence of sin remains, Satan continues to have a foothold within us which prevents us from being totally filled and empowered by God's Spirit. Much of our preaching is powerless rather than Spirit-empowered. Moreover, sin's influence upon us is evident to those that hear our words. The difference between our call for repentance from others and lack of personal repentance leaves our hearers in doubt. Our listeners fail to see the power of God's Word at work in us. Their impression is that either the words we are proclaiming are not true, or that we do not really believe the words ourselves. This unbelief results in a lack of repentance so that listeners remain in bondage to sin.

The proclamation of the gospel followed by the response of repentance brings about "forgiveness of sins" (Luke 24:47). The Greek word *aphesin* translated "forgiveness" means literally "to send away." The word picture is that of a prisoner released from his bondage and sent away to begin a new life.[33] This reminds us of the woman caught in the act of adultery to whom Jesus said, "Go now and leave your life of sin" (John 8:11). God's forgiveness enables a person to leave behind his or her slavery to sin to begin a new life.

While the result of the old life of sin is death, new life is God's eternal gift through Jesus Christ (Rom. 6:23). When God forgives a person, He removes the person's sin "as far as the east is from the west" (Ps. 103:12). God puts the person's sins behind God's back (Isa. 38:17) so that He does not remember them any more (Isa. 43:25).[34] As a result of God's forgiveness, our hearts become clean and pure (Isa. 1:18).

Jesus' death makes possible forgiveness of sin for the "whole world" (1 John 2:2). The Lord's will is for not "anyone to perish, but everyone come to repentance" (2 Pet. 3:9). Our commission is to proclaim the gospel so that "all nations" have the opportunity to experience this forgiveness (Luke 24:47). Nations are made up of individuals that need to experience the power of God's forgiveness. As we proclaim God's Word to these individuals that form the nations of the world, we give them the opportunity to respond in repentance and faith, releasing the power of God's forgiveness in their lives.

Where sin is present, Satan and his spirits exercise control in people's lives. When the work of Christ is applied to people's lives through repentance and forgiveness, they experience freedom from the power of evil.[35] The moment people "take God at His Word and believe" that Jesus' sacrifice was for their sins, they are set free from Satan's control.[36]

Call to Obedience

Jesus gathered with His disciples on a mountain in Galilee (Matt. 28:16-20). This was only a few days after the crucifixion and resurrection, and Jesus' followers displayed a range of responses based on the tumult they had just experienced. "When they saw him, they worshiped; but some doubted" (Matt. 28:17). The One who stood before them was the exalted Son of God in a glorified spiritual body. They could not help but worship Him. I am certain they felt much like Moses before the burning bush who sensed his inadequacy to carry out God's mission (Ex. 3:11; 4:1, 10). Or Isaiah whose encounter with God caused Isaiah to realize that he was "unclean" (Isa. 6:5). Or Saul on the road to Damascus who realized he had actually been fighting against God (Acts 9:1-5). Doubt crept in as Jesus' disciples confronted the reality of an unknown future. Because of what they had experienced, they would never be the same again, but what would they become? How would their lives be different because they had come face to face with God?

Jesus reminded His followers that He was in control, not only of the current situation, but of everything. Jesus said, "All authority on heaven and in earth has been given to me" (Matt. 28:18). Here was the "resurrected, exalted God-man, having entered upon His inheritance, announcing that full, supreme, total, pure power which He had from the beginning of the world is now granted to Him."[37] Jesus had control over not only the natural physical world, but also the supernatural spiritual world as well. His defeat of Satan and the forces of evil already was certain because of what Jesus had accomplished through His death and resurrection.[38]

Jesus' comprehensive authority over the universe extends to personal authority over His followers as well. As we have seen, those who have been saved from the dominion of Satan have come under the rule of Christ. This is what we mean when we say, "Jesus is Lord." Jesus exercises His authority by commanding His followers to "*make disciples* of all nations" (Matt. 28:19, emphasis added).[39]

The words *panta ta ethne* translated "all nations" in Matthew 28:19 was used by the Jews in the first century to refer to the Gentile nations.[40] Rather than nation-states in the modern sense, *nations* here refers to ethnic groups identifiable by means of shared language and culture. In this sense, the meaning is much closer to the word *tribe*. It also may be thought of in connection with other distinctive groupings of people, such as the castes of traditional Hinduism or subcultures in contemporary complex societies.[41] Jesus desires for people of every nation, language, culture, social class, and economic stratum to be His *disciples*.

The Greek word *mathetes* translated *disciple* means a person who is "involved in an intimate fellowship and relationship" with a "religious teacher" for the purpose of training the heart and will as well as the mind.[42] The training of a disciple goes beyond intellectual instruction and behavior modification. The disciple-maker cannot merely model appropriate words and actions in order to be mimicked by the person he or she is training.[43] Rather, the goal of discipleship must be a changed heart which will result in a genuine transformation of the will, motives, words and actions of the disciple.

In Matthew 28:19-20, Jesus gives a two-fold process for making disciples, *baptism* and *teaching*. *Baptism* is a "one-time, public witness . . . of allegiance to Christ."[44] It is both an initial "demonstration of faith in Christ" and a symbol of "incorporation into His Body, the Church" (1 Cor. 12:13).[45] The biblical pattern is repentance and faith in Christ followed as soon as possible by baptism (Acts 2:41; 8:12-13, 36-37; 9:17-18; 10:47-48; 16:14-15, 31-33; 18:8; 19:5).[46]

Save for the thief on the cross, the New Testament provides no example of a genuine believer in Jesus who was not baptized. This stands in stark contrast with today when "there are many who profess faith in and allegiance to the Lord Jesus Christ, but they have either not been baptized or they see no need to be baptized."[47] In many places, fifty to eighty percent of those who make decisions for Christ are never baptized. This results in ambiguity regarding their salvation and limits the possibility of future spiritual growth.[48]

Baptism is the new disciple's initial act of obedience to Christ. A person who is baptized establishes his or her "identity" as a "follower of Jesus Christ." This is a public testimony of the person's transfer of allegiance from the ruler of this world to King Jesus,[49] the Creator and rightful Ruler of the universe. Compromise on baptism tends to lead to disobedience in other areas of spiritual life. A person who is not willing to take this first step with Jesus will have difficulty following Him for a lifetime. Most people who refuse baptism within a short time become cut off from meaningful involvement with other Christians. This lack of interaction with other believers limits the possibility of experiencing God's grace at work within the Church.

Jesus said the discipleship process is completed by "teaching them to obey everything that I have commanded you" (Matt. 28:20). Discipleship cannot be done quickly. It is a "lifelong process" which has as its goal learning *to do everything Jesus commanded*. We must be careful not to limit discipleship to the accumulation of "Bible knowledge" or the development of "ministry skills."[50] Rather, the intended result is to actually reproduce the life of Jesus in the disciple, so that he or she becomes "mature, attaining to the whole measure of the fullness of Christ" (Eph.

4:13). Until a person assumes the character of Christ in thought, will, word and deed, the process of discipleship remains incomplete.

Jesus provides a three-fold definition of a mature *disciple* in John's Gospel. First, a *disciple* of Christ is committed to God's Word as a "reliable guide for daily living." Those who "hold to" Jesus' teaching are His real disciples (John 8:31). There is a firm commitment, not only to reading and understanding the Bible, but also to making biblical teaching the principles upon which all of the decisions of life are based. I remember a seminary professor once telling my class, "It makes little difference defining what the Bible is unless we are willing to act on what it says." Authentic Christian discipleship is characterized by a desire to live in accordance with God's Word.

Second, Jesus' *disciple* follows His example by laying down his or her life for others (John 13:34-35; 15:13). As the previous section emphasized, those who follow Jesus love others in the same way that they have been loved by Him (1 John 4:7-12).

Third, a *disciple* is one who "abides daily in fruit-bearing union with Christ" (John 15:4-5; Gal. 5:22-23). Through the work of His Spirit, Jesus reproduces His character in His *disciples.* This enables them to fully bear the words and actions of Christ to the world so that other people can both *see* and *hear* Christ through them.[51]

Every Christian, including every missionary, pastor and evangelist, is involved in the discipleship process on two levels. On one level, we are *making disciples.* We are leading others to faith in Christ and encouraging them to grow into spiritually mature followers of Jesus Christ. At the same time, all Christians are also *disciples in the making*. None have arrived at spiritual maturity. Often our words and deeds reflect merely a veiled shadow of the image of Christ. All are the "jars of clay" through whom God has chosen "to show this all-surpassing power" (2 Cor. 4:7). In many cases, we are no more than one or two steps ahead of the people we are training on the road to spiritual maturity. These one or two steps are enough to lead, but not enough to control.

In discipling relationships, it is never appropriate to act as though we have absolute spiritual authority or complete knowledge of spiritual truth. We do not want to train people to follow us. We want to train people to follow Jesus. We best accomplish this by living as humble servants who, by our example, show what it means to be a follower of Jesus Christ.

For a few years I served as a cooperating missionary with an established church in Japan. Over time, I noticed that the most influential person in this church was not the pastor, the missionaries, or the deacons. Rather, it was a little old lady who came faithfully to worship, prayed for the ministry of the church, and reached out in love to every person who came through the door. She brought many of these people through the door herself—people she had met in the neighborhood or on an errand in some other part of the city. She built relationships with them, encouraged them, did what she could to meet their needs, and prayed for them. She used every opportunity the Lord gave her to tell these people about Jesus. I watched as one after another of this dear saint's "projects" committed their lives to Christ, grew towards spiritual maturity and began to serve the Lord faithfully. This woman lived out Jesus' command to make disciples.

Spirit Empowered Witnesses

Acts 1:8 is about *Who* is in charge of Christian mission. This is a vital point often overlooked today. Churches and mission agencies now engage in strategic planning, designed to accomplish as much as possible with the limited resources available. Much attention is given to focusing personnel, financial and ministry resources in strategic locations. This may mean emphasizing areas of greater responsiveness or, alternatively, unreached people groups. In this present day context, the application of Acts 1:8 is that of the Spirit empowering *us* to do mission. We become the primary *actors* in mission and the Holy Spirit is reduced to our primary *equipment* for the completion of the task.

In the original context of Acts 1:8, planning did take place. The leaders in Jerusalem devoted themselves to teaching the Word while others were appointed for the ministry of service (Acts 6:1-7). Paul decided to proclaim the gospel and start churches primarily among the Gentiles. He made plans to travel to Rome on his way to Spain (Rom. 15:24). However, these plans were always open to correction and adjustment. In each stage we find that the One in control was not Paul or the apostolic leadership of the church in

Jerusalem. The One in control was the Holy Spirit. The Holy Spirit set the agenda and then worked through the Church to accomplish God's mission.

Jesus' statement in Acts 1:8 was in response to His disciples' question about God's authority and God's plan. The disciples asked, "Lord, are you at this time going to restore the kingdom of Israel?" (Acts 1:6) Jesus' resurrection fueled the disciples' hopes for the restoration of Israel. They sought a geo-political kingdom, led by a restored Davidic monarchy, which would finally free itself of Roman rule.[52]

The desire to politicize God's kingdom and His mission in the world is still with us. According to this view, *salvation* is liberation from political oppression and *evangelism* is "participation in the battle for a more just social order."[53] This kind of ideology substitutes economic evolution and political revolution for spiritual transformation, and is a distortion of Christ's mission in the world.[54]

Jesus said, "My kingdom is not of this world. If it were my servants would fight . . . But now my kingdom is from another place" (John 18:36). Jesus' intention was to bring about a *spiritual kingdom* in which His rule would replace that of Satan, the "prince of this world" (John 12:31; 14:30; 16:11). This kingdom is to be brought in through a *spiritual method,* the proclamation of the good news of Jesus Christ through the words and actions of God's people, the Church.[55] The proclamation of the gospel brings about faith in Christ, and this faith brings the freedom which people seek. "The whole world is a prisoner of sin, so that what was promised, being given through faith in Jesus Christ, might be given to those who believe" (Gal. 3:22).

Jesus reminded His disciples of *His Father's authority* over the events of history (Acts 1:7). History is divided into periods of time distinguished by critical events which shape its course. God exercises ultimate control over both history and the events which shape it.[56] God chose to intervene in history decisively by sending His Son at a specific moment, to a specific place, among a specific people, as a specific person.[57] Yet God's intervention in history in Jesus Christ was for the "whole world" (1 John 2:2), for "everyone who believes in him" (John 3:16).

God extends His authority into the whole world through the power of the Holy Spirit. "You will receive power when the Holy Spirit comes on you" (Acts 1:8). Since the Holy Spirit is God's Spirit (Joel 2:28; 1 Cor. 2:11; 2 Cor. 1:21-22; 5:5; Gal. 3:5; 1 Thes. 4:8), the power of the Holy Spirit is God's own power and authority which He has bestowed upon His people to accomplish His mission in the world. Through the Spirit, God Himself "dwells" among His people, so that both individually (1 Cor. 3:16) and corporately (1 Pet. 2:5), they become God's temple.[58] Gordon Fee writes,

> The Spirit is God's own personal presence in our lives and in our midst, who leads us into paths of righteousness for his own name's sake, who "is working all things in all people," and who is grieved when his

> people do not reflect his character and thus reveal his glory.[59]

The Witness is the Holy Spirit. Jesus said, "When the Counselor comes, whom I will send to you from the Father, the Spirit of truth who goes out from the Father, he will testify about me" (John 15:26). The Spirit comes to bear witness to the world regarding Jesus Christ (John 16:13-15). The Spirit is in control of the proclamation of the Gospel, the growth of the Church, and the expansion of God's kingdom. All of these tasks, which we so often choose to take upon our own shoulders, are His mission. He is in charge and we are His tools, to the extent that we allow the Spirit to work through us. The Holy Spirit desires to use us as His means to carry out His mission of bearing witness for Christ.

The power of the Holy Spirit produces evangelistic witness through us. God's Spirit "overpowers" the human will, subjugating the person to His control.[60] God's Spirit exercises God's rule in and through His people.[61] When this occurs, the Holy Spirit causes the person to bear witness for Christ.

As in Matthew 28, Mark 16 and Luke 24, in Acts 1:8 Christians are to witness to all of the nations of the world. Witness extends through a geographic expansion beginning at Jerusalem, moves out to "all of Judea and Samaria," and continues to the "ends of the earth." This description is a step by step description of the expansion of the gospel in the book of Acts.[62] Yet it also provides a directive that every Christian should follow in carrying out our Lord's command to be His witnesses.

I am still amazed that God chose a boy from a small town in northeast Texas and sent him to share the gospel in Tokyo, Japan. While I have a heart for reaching the world my witness must always be *local*. Whether I am in Texas or in Tokyo, I bear witness *to those I live among* of God's love in Jesus Christ, calling them to salvation through faith in Him.

Every Christian is called to begin mission at *Jerusalem*, bearing witness for Christ in his or her own community. We continue to be *local witnesses* throughout our lives, whether we continue to live in the communities where we were born and reared, relocate to a nearby community *(Judea)*, to a neighboring state *(Samaria)*, or to the other side of the world.

The key to reaching the world for Christ is making disciples *where we live*. This is because only growing disciples working through healthy local churches are able to carry the gospel to the ends of the earth.[63] When we invest our time making disciples who are obedient to our Lord's commands, we produce Christians who are capable of carrying out the Great Commission.[64] Growing Christians reproduce themselves, leading to the multiplication of disciples and churches. This provides the leadership necessary to make disciples among all the nations of the world.[65] This type of "spiritual multiplication through disciple-making" is the only effective means of "reaching the world for Christ."[66]

Making Disciples: God's Strategy for Reaching the Nations

For many years missionaries who served in Japan emphasized that, in spite of sluggish growth, Christianity in Japan played a strategic place in world missions. The argument went that Japan was the leading economic and political power in East Asia. Geographically, culturally and technologically, Japan stood at the crossroads between East and West. If the Japanese people could be led to faith in Christ, then Japan's position and resources could be used for the advance of Christianity throughout Asia. In this regard, Japan was regarded as the key to the Orient: as Japan went so went Asia.

At the present time, Japan has not materialized as the key to the spread of the gospel in Asia. While church growth has continued to move forward at a snail's pace in Japan, in other areas of East Asia Christianity is advancing like a racing rabbit. Other nations, such as South Korea, China and the Philippines, have taken the lead in reaching Asia with the gospel. South Korea is now second to only the United States in the number of missionaries sent out for service in other countries. Through the "Back to Jerusalem Movement," the house churches of China have a goal of sending out over 100,000 missionaries in the next few years.[67] Since the 1970's, over 40,000 new evangelical churches have been planted in the Philippines.[68] Each year thousands of Filipinos fan out across Asia to work, not as missionaries, but as domestic workers and in other menial positions. Filipino Christians who penetrate the households and companies of East Asia, South Asia and the Middle East, are in position to share the gospel with many who have never even met a Christian much less heard the good news of Jesus Christ. As these Filipino Christians share their faith with their employers and fellow-workers, they are making disciples in places a missionary could never enter.

When we look at Korea, China and the Philippines, we come to understand that God's strategy for reaching the world is not about money, social influence or political clout. In each of these countries there are firmly established churches committed to proclaiming the gospel and training believers to obey Christ's commands. People who experience the transforming power of God's Word become energized for mission.

God's strategy for the advance of His kingdom is based upon people. God's kingdom grows as people trust in Christ, become His obedient followers, and then go into the world to bear witness to the gospel through words and actions. Those who bear witness encourage others to trust in Christ, teach them to obey the commands of Christ, and then send them out to make disciples. As the cycle continues, the number of disciples multiplies, the Church grows, and God's kingdom pushes back the kingdom of darkness.

Our part in this process is to invest our lives in people. We must share Jesus' love with them until they, like the apostle John, come to the conclusion, "Jesus loves even *me*," and commit their lives and eternities to Him. Then we are to encourage them to become like Jesus, loving others in word and deed so that the light of Christ shines through them into a world made dark by the stain of sin. As they grow towards Christian maturity, they will lead others to faith in Christ and be able to disciple them as well.

God is in control. He is at work through His Son, His Spirit and His Church to bring the people of all nations to Himself. Since God has absolute power and authority, the completion of God's strategy is certain. All we need to do is to obey His Word.

Understanding and Applying God's Word

1. ***Why have many people not experienced the impact of the gospel?***
2. ***What did Jesus mean when He commanded His followers to make disciples?***
3. ***What are some of the personal costs that may be involved in making disciples?***
4. ***How does unforgiven sin allow Satan to have a foothold in people's lives?***
5. ***What is the relationship between repentance and forgiveness?***
6. ***What is the significance of baptism in the Christian life?***
7. ***What are some characteristics of a mature disciple?***
8. ***Who is in charge of Christian mission?***
9. ***What is our role in Christian mission?***

CHAPTER FIVE

"YOU SHALL BE MY WITNESSES"

A new age dawned with coming of the Holy Spirit. During this period, often referred to as the *Age of the Church* or the *Age of the Spirit,* the Holy Spirit applies the power of God's Word to people of all nations, bringing them the "benefits and blessings" of the "death, resurrection and ascension" of Jesus Christ.[1] The Holy Spirit empowers Jesus' followers to proclaim God's Word. God's Spirit works in partnership with these witnesses, confirming the truth of the gospel in the hearers' hearts (1 Cor. 2:4)[2] so they are able to respond with repentance and faith. God's Word advances in the power of the Spirit, breaking down human barriers and advancing God's kingdom among the nations.

We should have the same Spirit-empowered witness for Jesus Christ that characterized His first disciples in the book of Acts. We have met the resurrected, exalted Christ. We have bowed our knees to Him and called Him, "Lord." Jesus has sent His Spirit to live within us as His personal presence. When the Spirit's power breathes Christ's life into us,

He re-creates us in Christ's image and compels us to make Christ known.

Proclaiming Jesus

During the first century, believers in Judaism from every part of the Mediterranean world (Acts 2:5, 9-11) gathered in Jerusalem for the celebration of Pentecost.[3] They were astounded to hear Galileans speaking so that each person heard the "wonders of God . . . in his own native language" (Acts 2:8, 12). "What does this mean? Are these men drunk?" they asked (Acts 2:13, 14). They were unable to comprehend the working of God's Spirit. The acts of Jesus' disciples on Pentecost were not the irrational results of alcoholic intoxication, but rather the supernatural results of the Holy Spirit's inspiration.

Peter told the crowd they were seeing the fulfillment of God's promise through the prophet Joel (Joel 2:28-32; Acts 2:16-21). Jesus, whom they had crucified, had been resurrected and "exalted to the right hand of God" (Acts 2:23, 33). This same Jesus now exalted as "both Lord and Christ" (Acts 2:36), "poured out" the "promised Holy Spirit" (Acts 2:33). Peter said what they saw and heard was the result of Christ Himself at "work in their midst."[4] W. T. Conner points to the fundamental importance of this identification of the Spirit's work with the work of Christ,

> This assures that anything done out of harmony with the character of Christ is not really done in the power of the Holy Spirit, no matter what the doer may claim.

> This makes Jesus—his life, character and spirit—the fundamental test that should be applied to any work wrought as in the power of the Holy Spirit. If the result does not square with the known character and work of Jesus Christ, it cannot be recognized as produced by the Spirit of God. God does not work a work of one spiritual quality through Jesus and a different quality by the Holy Spirit.[5]

A short time later, Peter and John were going to the temple when they passed a crippled man. This man who had been "crippled from birth" begged everyday at the temple (Acts 3:2). Jesus and His disciples may have passed this man many times. They even may have given him money. But until this time Jesus had not healed him. The Great Physician healed so many, but left this man lame and lying at the temple gate. It was not that Jesus and His disciples were unconcerned about his physical condition. God planned to use this man's healing for a greater purpose.

This is an example of how God orchestrates events in order to accomplish His purpose. If Jesus had healed the man earlier, there may have been little response other than wonder and amazement. Increased animosity on the part of the Jerusalem religious establishment also may have occurred. But when this man was healed, Peter proclaimed the gospel with the result that thousands of people turned to faith in Christ.

When Peter said, "Look at us!" the crippled man expected to receive money (Acts 3:4-5). The man did not expect to be healed. He had been lame since birth. He thought he would spend his whole life as a crippled beggar lying at the temple gate.

There are many people who believe they are trapped in their present life without any hope of change. They are in bondage—physically, psychologically or spiritually. They are unaware of God's power to free them. So when we come to them with good news of the free gift of salvation through Jesus Christ, there is a tendency on their part to discount God's offer made through us as little more than a fairy tale or wishful thinking. How can a person really leave his or her old way of life behind and begin again?

Peter healed the crippled man "in the name of Jesus Christ" (Acts 3:6). Peter was not in control, using Jesus' name as a supernatural tool in order to bring about healing. Rather, Peter spoke as one acting under the authority of Jesus Christ.[6] Peter's words introduced the power of Christ, God's living Word, into this man's life. It was Jesus' power exercised through Peter that made the crippled man whole (Acts 3:16).

Peter believed Jesus could heal this man because Peter had seen Jesus heal others. He also had experienced Jesus' healing power in his own life. In Peter's case the healing was not physical, but the much deeper spiritual wounds that resulted from his denial of Christ. Peter believed that the Jesus who had healed Peter's heart also could heal the crippled man's feet. Acting upon this faith, Peter spoke words which brought healing.[7]

An "astonished" crowd gathered to see this man, lame for more than forty years, now "walking and praising God" (Acts 3:9-11; 4:22). Peter proclaimed Jesus to them. As in

Acts 2, Peter's message was that they had rejected and killed Jesus, but God raised Him from the dead (Acts 3:13-15). Peter told the crowd that through faith in Jesus the crippled man had been healed (Acts 3:16).

The apostle concluded his message: "Repent, then, and turn to God" (Acts 3:19). He called on them to turn from rejection of Christ to faith in Christ. Three results were promised: their sins will be "wiped out", "refreshing will come from the Lord," and they will be restored as God's people (Acts 3:19-23).[8] Peter told his listeners that their status as God's people did not depend on physical descent from Abraham. It depended, rather, on their willingness to hear and to obey God's Word. Those who received God's Word would participate in His kingdom, but those who rejected it would be "cut off" (Acts 3:22-23). Faith in God's Word brings about not only healing but also cleansing from sin, spiritual refreshing and a renewed relationship with Him.[9]

When Peter and John were brought before the ruling council, Peter was "filled with the Holy Spirit" and began to speak boldly (Acts 4:8). The Spirit's filling produced the Word's proclamation.[10] Peter and John not only *wanted* to talk about Jesus, they were *compelled* to talk about Him. They said, "We cannot help speaking . . ." (Acts 4:20). There were three reasons that Peter and John had to talk about Jesus. First, as noted by the Jewish leaders, "these men had been with Jesus" (Acts 4:13). Second, Peter and John believed they must obey God rather than succumbing to the desires of other people (Acts 4:19). God had commanded them to be His witnesses, and He had filled them with His Spirit for this purpose. This command came from the One who has ultimate authority over the whole universe (Matt. 28:18-20). They had to obey eternal, almighty God rather than mortal men. Third, they had to talk about what they had experienced (Acts 4:20). "They had been eyewitnesses to the ministry of Christ and above all his resurrection appearances. No one could prevent them from preaching what they knew to be true."[11] They had experienced Christ's power to heal, to forgive, to refresh with His Spirit, to make new. This experience brought such exuberance that they could not hold it in.

God guides the process of evangelization, both globally by sending His witnesses to the nations, and individually by giving those with prepared hearts the opportunity to hear His Word and believe. For example, God orchestrated the encounter between Philip and the Ethiopian eunuch from first to last (Acts 8:26-40). God sent an angel to tell Philip to go to the Jerusalem-Gaza road. Philip was in the midst of a great spiritual awakening in Samaria, so it would have been easy to hesitate and question God's leadership. He could have asked, "Why leave an area of great responsiveness to go somewhere else?" But when God told Philip to go, he left immediately (Acts 8:26-27).

When Philip saw the Ethiopian eunuch riding in his chariot, the Spirit told Philip to go to the chariot (Acts 8:28-30). Notice Philip's obedience. An official of high status would not have traveled alone. The eunuch must have had an entourage of guards, messengers and secretaries accompanying him on his journey. Philip did not stop to consider, "What will all of these people think if I approach this man's chariot?" When the Spirit spoke, Philip ran (Acts 8:30).

While God was getting Philip in position to share the gospel, He also was preparing the Ethiopian's heart to receive the message. Long before, the eunuch had come in contact with Judaism. Through the study of God's Word, he had come to believe there was one true God, the Creator of heaven and earth. He became a worshiper of this God. This eunuch had taken time from work and traveled several hundred miles to worship in Jerusalem, even though he could not enter the temple. Now, as he began his journey home, he read the words of Isaiah 53:7-8 and contemplated their meaning,

> He was led like a sheep to the slaughter, and as a lamb before the shearer is silent, so he did not open his mouth. In his humiliation he was deprived of justice. Who can speak of his descendants? For his life was taken from the earth (Acts 8:32-33).

It is an understatement to say the eunuch was ready to hear the gospel. When Philip told him about Jesus, the eunuch believed immediately. He was baptized on the spot as a public testimony to those in his entourage of his faith in Jesus Christ (Acts 8:35-36).[12] This man who was unable to have his own family became a member of God's family (John 1:12-13). Although excluded from entering the temple in Jerusalem, the eunuch entered the "spiritual house" that God is building based upon the foundation of His Son, Jesus Christ (1 Pet. 2:4-5).[13]

Notice the *evangelistic strategy* used to reach this important Ethiopian official for Christ. In contrast with some of the complex strategies of the twenty-first century, the strategy employed here was quite simple. First, Philip *obeyed God's leadership.* When God spoke, Philip acted. He neither hesitated nor ran ahead of God. Rather, Philip had such an awareness of God's voice that he was able to act in perfect timing with God's plan.

Second, Philip *proclaimed the "good news of Jesus"* (Acts 8:35). He began where the eunuch was, in Isaiah 53, and proceeded from that point to share Christ with him. Everyone the Spirit leads to us will not be so far along the path to salvation as the eunuch was. They may not be ready to place their faith in Jesus right then and there. But wherever they are spiritually, we need to begin at that point and to help them make their next step towards faith in Jesus Christ.

Hearing is just as important as speaking for evangelism. In order to be effective in sharing God's Word, we must learn to listen to both the Spirit's voice and the words of those with whom we are sharing. A few years ago, my wife asked a Japanese friend to whom she was witnessing, "What do *you* believe?" The friend responded, "I have known missionaries for twenty years, but you are the first one that ever asked me what I thought." What an indicting statement. This woman had been closed to Christianity because she had been treated like a target rather than a person. Now, for the first time, she sensed that she really was valued and cared for. She became more open to hear my wife's witness. Also, my wife could witness more effectively because, after listening, she could respond to her friend's specific issues.

A missionary traveling across Tokyo by train saw a Japanese young man sitting across from him reading a Bible. The missionary sensed that the Spirit was saying to him, "You need to speak to that man. He is your *Ethiopian eunuch!"* As the man rose to get off the train, the missionary jumped up and followed him. As they got off the train, the missionary said, "I noticed that you were reading a Bible. Are you interested in English?" The young man responded, "No. I'm interested in the Bible." The missionary made an appointment to meet the man the next day so they could talk together. As the man walked away, the missionary gave him a tract. The missionary hoped the man would look over the tract so they could use it as a basis for conversation when they met the next day.

It did not go as the missionary planned. When they sat down together, the young man pulled out the tract, turned to the last page, and pointed to the sinner's prayer. He said, "This says that if I pray this prayer I can receive Christ. Can I do this *now?"* This young man had lived with a Christian family in the United States. He had heard the Bible and, just as importantly, he had seen the family live out the truth of God's Word everyday. Then, when the timing was right, God sent his messenger to lead this man to faith in Jesus Christ. This would not have happened if the missionary had hesitated. God was able to use him because of his obedience. When God spoke he moved.

Evangelism is not a human-driven strategy. It was not Philip's strategy that resulted in the Ethiopian eunuch turning to faith in Christ. And it was not a missionary strategy that led to this young man's salvation. In both cases, the strategy included human instruments, but the people were not in charge. The strategy was God's strategy. God's strategy is to lead us to those He has prepared to hear God's Word. When we are sensitive to the leadership of God's Spirit and faithful to share His Word, God uses our witness to lead people to faith in Christ.

Breaking Down Human Barriers

God removes barriers in order to accomplish His mission of making disciples of all the nations. These barriers include language, culture, and ethnicity, as well as economic and social status. There are areas of resistance among those we are trying to persuade to come to faith in Christ, such as immorality, pride and idolatry. The hearts of Christians also may contain barriers to the advance of the gospel. Our own pride and prejudices may stand in the way of God accomplishing what He desires through us.

In Acts 2, Jesus' followers proclaimed God's Word so the multitude that heard their message repented of their sins and turned to faith in Christ. The Holy Spirit bore witness through the disciples to call people to faith in Christ. God's promises of forgiveness and the gift of the Spirit are "for all who are far off—for all whom the Lord our God will call" (Acts 2:39). The people of every nation who believe in Jesus Christ receive these gifts.[14] When there is authentic faith in

Christ, there always will be forgiveness and spiritual transformation.

On the Day of Pentecost, the Holy Spirit worked through the proclamation of God's Word to break down human barriers such as nationalism, language and culture. People from all parts of the Roman Empire assembled in Jerusalem were amazed to hear the "wonders of God" proclaimed in their own languages (Acts 2:5-11). At the Tower of Babel (Gen. 11:1-9), the people were scattered throughout the earth by the confusion of language because of their disobedience to God's command. On Pentecost, the "curse of Babel" was reversed as the "language barrier [was] supernaturally overcome." This demonstrated the "multi-racial, multi-national, multi-lingual nature of the kingdom of Christ."[15]

God's Spirit was poured out "on all people" (Acts 2:17), regardless of age, gender or social class, clarifying that salvation through Jesus Christ is equally available to all who believe in Him.[16] As Paul writes, "There is neither Jew nor Greek, slave nor free, male nor female, for you are all one in Christ Jesus" (Gal. 3:28).

The gospel witness advanced beyond the Jews to other peoples, beginning with those who already had some belief in the true God. Peter was a typical first century Jew, brought up to believe that certain foods and certain people were unclean. Even after he became a Christian, the persistence of these former beliefs prevented Peter from eating unclean animals, and prevented him from interacting with Gentiles. God used a dramatic vision to remove this barrier from Peter's heart so that he could witness to Gentiles. In Peter's vision, three times a large sheet from heaven was let down to earth. On this sheet were all kinds of animals, reptiles and birds, including many that Jews considered inedible. God said three times, "Get up, Peter. Kill and eat." Peter argued against God, "Surely not, Lord! I have never eaten anything impure or unclean." Then God said, "Do not call anything impure that God has made clean" (Acts 10:11-15).

Jewish custom made it taboo for Peter to enter the house of a Gentile,[17] but God's revelation took precedence over these human customs (Acts 10:28). When invited by messengers to go to Cornelius' house, Peter obeyed the Spirit's command to go with them without hesitation (Acts 10:20). Peter learned that "God does not show favoritism but accepts men from every nation who fear him and do what is right" (Acts 10:34-35). Peter's spiritual transformation enabled him to preach the gospel in Cornelius' house.[18]

When called upon to speak to Cornelius and his household, Peter preached that there is "peace through Jesus Christ, who is Lord of all" (Acts 10:36). Peter's message reflected the insight of fresh revelation. Whereas formerly he thought of Jesus as the Jewish Messiah, Peter now realized Jesus came to be Lord and Savior of the *whole world*. God does not want "*anyone* to perish, but *everyone* to come to repentance" (2 Pet. 3:9, emphasis added). Through Christ, the former wall of separation between Jew and Gentile has been torn down. As Paul writes, "God was reconciling the world to himself in Christ" (2 Cor. 5:19).

Peter's message at Cornelius' house emphasized three points. First, the Holy Spirit empowered Jesus for "healing all who were under the power of the devil" (Acts 10:38). The same Spirit who empowered Jesus now empowered Peter to proclaim the gospel.[19] And the work of this same Spirit enabled Cornelius and his family to experience forgiveness of sins and eternal life.[20]

His second point was that he and the other apostles were eyewitnesses of Jesus' death and resurrection (Acts 10:39-41). They had a special qualification to proclaim the gospel because they had "witnessed Jesus' ministry from baptism through the resurrection appearances."[21] Their testimony of Christ was based on firsthand experience rather than second-hand information.

Although this specific qualification for proclamation was unique to the first apostles, there is a sense in which it is true for us as well. Jesus said, "Blessed are those who have not seen and yet have believed" (John 20:29). Unless we have met Jesus spiritually and experience a daily, vital relationship with Him, our testimony for Christ will have an empty ring. Our proclamation of the gospel must communicate that the Jesus of the Scriptures has changed our lives. Our relationship with Jesus should affect what we think and feel and do everyday. Whether or not this is true will be obvious to those with whom we attempt to share our faith. George and Woodbridge write,

> People are not able to peer into our hearts. Unbelievers cannot know the true status of our relationship with God. But

> they can hear our words and see our lives. And on the basis of what they observe, Jesus said, they have a right to draw a conclusion about our faith in Christ. . . Words must be followed by deeds, costly deeds that demonstrate the highest standard possible or imaginable. It is the standard of Jesus' own love for us.[22]

Jesus demonstrated this standard when He put aside His divine status, took the form of a humble servant and died on a Roman cross (Phil. 2:5-8). In order to follow Jesus' example, Peter laid aside his prejudice against the Gentiles in order to share the gospel with Cornelius and his family.

Third, Peter said he obeyed Jesus' command to preach so that those who believed in Christ could "receive forgiveness of sins through his name" (Acts 10:42-43). Forgiveness of sins came, not as a result of becoming a Jew or obeying the law, but through faith in Christ.[23] As Paul writes, both Jews and Gentiles are "justified by faith in Christ and not by observing the law" (Gal. 2:15, 16). The people of "all nations" are saved through faith in Christ (Gal. 3:6, 9, 26-29). When Cornelius and those gathered with him heard Peter's words, the Holy Spirit opened their hearts so that they were able grasp the message, repent of their sins, and believe in Jesus.[24]

The Holy Spirit came upon *all* who heard Peter's message (Acts 10:44). *All* of them believed in Jesus, and *all* experienced spiritual regeneration. Then *all* were baptized as a public testimony of their salvation (Acts 10:44-47). The other Jewish believers who had come with Peter realized these Gentiles had received the gift of the Holy Spirit because they heard them "speaking in tongues and praising God" (Acts 10:46). Since God accepted the Gentile believers' faith, they must accept the validity of Gentile faith in Christ as well.[25] As Peter later told the leaders of the church assembled in Jerusalem, "If God gave them the same gift as he gave us, who believed in the Lord Jesus Christ, who was I to think that I could oppose God" (Acts 11:17).

God desires to break down the walls of alienation that result from sin. He not only is concerned about human alienation from God. He also is concerned about breaking down the walls of alienation between people. God accomplishes this purpose through people empowered by God's Spirit to proclaim His Word. Dennis Johnson writes,

> It is comfortable to stay in the sphere of people like ourselves, seeking refuge in a familiar ghetto of Christian contacts. But we cannot wait for non-Christians to cross the culture gaps, to scale the walls to get to know us well enough to see Christ's grace in our lives. The gospel speaks with power in every culture, to every people under heaven. When the gospel touches a new culture, it does not leave that culture unchanged. Yet God does not demand that people leave their culture to hear of his grace in Christ. We who have experienced this grace are the ones who must climb the walls, build the bridges, and suffer the stresses of culture shock. People who know Jesus must pay the price to pierce the barriers between peoples. And as they do,

> Jesus spreads his salvation to the ends of the earth.[26]

We communicate the truth of the gospel powerfully when we cross manmade barriers to go to those others consider unlovable—the terminally ill, those whose language, culture or religion that differ from our own, the rich and the poor, and those society regards as immoral and unclean. People transformed by God's Word believe He has the power to help others as well. They bear witness for Christ based on this faith in Him.

Joanne Shetler and Patricia Purvis write about the Balangao tribesmen in the Philippines who were headhunters.[27] The Balangaos sacrificed to evil spirits that controlled their lives.[28] The missionaries told them that Jesus Christ has greater power than the evil spirits. At first there was doubt because these were only the words of outsiders. But eventually, one by one, the Balangaos began to hear "God's voice" for themselves.[29] As the people believed, the evil spirits lost control over them.[30] "God defeated the spirits so dramatically and so often that [they] came to expect the miraculous."[31] The authors conclude, "The Word of God changes people. The more the Balangaos studied and learned, the more they changed."[32]

Sometimes it is more difficult to cross the tracks than it is to fly around the world. This is a problem for Christians in many areas of the world. I have been in churches in the southern United States that preach world missions, but reject African Americans who apply for membership. Churches in Japan often become uncomfortable when people from China,

Korea or the Philippines begin to attend. In many cases, churches in Africa are formed along tribal lines. And in India there are cases where caste distinctions may limit church membership.

God's plan is not only to cleanse our sins that separate us from God, but also to remove those sins that prevent us from having fellowship with one another.[33] While we must present the gospel to people in their own language and culture so that they can understand and believe, we must not let them remain where they are. When churches are made up of people from only one language, culture and socio-economic class, the possibility of the kind "mixing" the New Testament calls for seems remote.[34] When people are only comfortable worshipping with their "own kind of people," it is a mark of spiritual immaturity. The Holy Spirit moves us to embrace everyone who has bowed their knee at the foot of the cross.

We must take responsibility to cross barriers that divide human beings in order to make Christ known. Not only must we cross oceans, climb mountains and penetrate jungles for the sake of Christ. We must also cross the more insurmountable barriers of human pride and prejudice to carry the love of Jesus to those who do not know Him. We must allow Christ's Spirit to penetrate to the innermost part of our souls so that Christ's love will prevail in us.

Overcoming Spiritual Resistance

The proclamation of God's Word brings us into conflict with spiritual opposition. Sin is the devil's stronghold. God wants to break down these walls. Every person belongs to Him. Through His Son, God both made us and bought us. He continues to prod and push and knock (Rev. 3:20). God does this in partnership with His people through the preaching of the gospel and the inner working of His Spirit.

Philip proclaimed the gospel to the Samaritans, using both word and deed to call them to repentance and faith in Christ (Acts 8:4-12). Prior to Philip's arrival in Samaria, Simon Magus boasted of his own greatness (Acts 8:9), and the people deified and followed him (Acts 8:10-11). Since the worship of Simon was an act of *idolatry*, in which the worship of a created thing was substituted for worship of the Creator (Rom. 1:21-23), we can infer that demonic influence was at work, enabling Simon to perform magic deeds that bolstered his claims to deity.[35] Simon followed Satan's example of deceiving others so that they would worship him rather than the true God.[36]

When Philip came, he "proclaimed the Christ" to the Samaritans (Acts 8:5) and acted on Christ's authority to heal and cast out evil spirits (Acts 8:7). Many believed in Jesus Christ and were baptized (Acts 8:11-12). The Samaritans responded in faith because they saw an authenticity in Philip's preaching that was lacking in the words and wonders of Simon Magus. As a result of Simon's influence, demonic spirits held them in bondage. But through Philip's proclamation, Christ's power set the Samaritans free.[37]

Even Simon "believed and was baptized" (Acts 8:13). But Simon's faith was spurious because he thought the difference between his power and Jesus' power was a *difference of degree.* Simon did not recognize that Jesus' power was a *different kind* of power because it flowed from a *different source.* Simon's power came from Satan and brought about evil, suffering, despair and death. Jesus' power comes from God and produces life, good, righteousness and hope.

Simon revealed his true spiritual condition when he offered to buy the power to bestow the Holy Spirit through the laying on of hands (Acts 8:18-19). While professing to be a Christian, Simon actually believed that Philip, Peter and John were sorcerers. He believed that Peter and John could control the Holy Spirit, just as Simon controlled the spirits that did his magic. Simon reasoned this spiritual power also could be bought.[38] Simon wanted to manipulate and control God.[39] In attempting to usurp divine authority, Simon followed the leadership of his master Satan who wants to rule in place of God.[40]

We must guard against the tendency to "Simonize" God's Spirit. We are tempted to use prayer and worship as magical formulae to attempt to control the Spirit. Or we may try to *buy* the Spirit's power through the sacrificial giving of money, ability or just plain hard work. Human strategies cannot control the Spirit's action.

Peter told Simon to repent in order to receive God's forgiveness. Simon needed to repent because he was a "captive to sin" (Acts 8:22-23). Although Simon was acting under demonic influence, Peter did not expel these evil spirits. Rather, he pointed Simon to the source of his spiritual bondage—sin. If Simon would repent of his sin and turn to faith in Christ, the evil strongholds in his life would be broken down.

Paul and Barnabas encountered spiritual opposition through a Jewish "sorcerer and false prophet" in Paphos named Bar-Jesus or Elymas (Acts 13:6). The Greek word *magus* translated "sorcerer" is the very same word used for the *magi* in Matthew 2. It was used to describe someone who had special power through their knowledge of the stars, what we refer to as an astrologer.[41] Ben Witherington explains that Bar-Jesus was a diviner who through various rituals claimed to be able to evoke the dead, including the shades or spirits of one's ancestors. The use of the word "prophet" suggests that Elymas claimed to be able to tell the future, perhaps through necromancy, perhaps through astrology, or magical spells and rituals involving both.[42]

The confrontation that took place when Paul and Barnabas attempted to share the gospel with the Roman provincial governor, Sergius Paulus (Acts 13:7), was a conflict between God and Satan carried out through their emissaries.[43] It was a struggle between the powers of God's truth and satanic deception.

This kind of encounter takes place daily in places where the gospel is proclaimed to those that invoke the spiritual power of their ancestors. Ancestral practices are just as much a part of the contemporary Asian context as they were the New Testament world.

The New Testament never encourages praying to other human beings, either past family members or present rulers. Christians in the

Roman Empire actually were charged with *atheism* because they refused to participate in ancestral practices and emperor worship.

Paul told Elymas he was a "child of the devil" who used "all kinds of deceit and trickery" in order to pervert the "right ways of the Lord" (Acts 13:10). Bar-Jesus was carrying out Satan's plan to obstruct God's Word in order to prevent the Roman governor from turning to faith in Christ.[44] Paul dealt with Elymas "based [Paul's] authority in Christ,"[45] by proclaiming God's Word: "Now the hand of the Lord is against you. You are going to be blind, and for a time you will be unable to see the light of the sun" (Acts 13:11). The blinding of Elymas was part of Paul's proclamation of God's Word and made it clear to the Roman proconsul that Jesus had the power to defeat Satan. Sergius Paulus placed his faith in Christ because "he was amazed at the teaching about the Lord" (Acts 13:12).

We must be careful to observe the relationship between Satan's work and the belief systems of the people with whom we share God's Word. Satan uses the world's religions as vehicles to twist the truth in order to prevent people from trusting in Christ. There is an element of truth in every religion, but this embedded particle of veracity constitutes their danger. This element of truth, twisted by Satan, often prevents people from coming to faith in Christ.

While every culture includes elements that can be used to help explain the gospel, this is not the same thing as the assertion that Christ can be found through other religions. I am unaware of a single case in which explicit faith in another religion led directly to faith in Christ. But I have seen many cases in which commitment to another religion prevented a person from trusting in Jesus.

When I was in Japan, I never heard anyone say, "My Buddhist faith led me to believe in Jesus," but I often have been told, "I cannot become a Christian *because* I am a Buddhist." Those who make such statements have grasped the truth that turning to faith in Christ necessarily includes turning *from* Buddhism. Their commitment to Buddhism, whether due to personal faith or a family commitment, prevents a commitment to Christ.

Paul was in Philippi proclaiming the gospel, bringing people to faith in Christ, and planting a new church. One day he met a slave girl possessed by an evil spirit that enabled her to predict the future (Acts 16:16). The literal translation here is "Python spirit." Unger tells us,

> In Greek mythology, "Python" (Puthon) was the name of the mythical dragon, that dwelt in the vicinity of Pytho, at the foot of Mount Parnassus, in Phocis. It was said to have been the guardian of the most famous of all Greek oracles at Delphi, and to have been slain by Apollo . . . Consequently, "the Pythian spirit" . . . was tantamount to a "divining demon" . . . and, in the course of time, came to be the generic title of the supposed source of diviners in general, including the slave girl, whom Satan used at Philippi to oppose the truth of the gospel.[46]

The influence of the Python spirit brought about "satanically empowered" prophetic utterances.[47] There certainly is a "Python Spirit" at work in the occult, the cults, and other religions. But this serpent was not slain by Apollo. Rather, it is the "great dragon . . . that ancient serpent called the devil, or Satan, who leads the whole world astray" (Rev. 12:9).

The slave girl shouted, "These men are servants of the Most High God, who are telling you the way to be saved" (Acts 16:17). An evil spirit led the girl to say something which sounded like orthodox Christianity. However, in Philippi's polytheistic setting, "Most High God" could be associated with any god that a person considered to be *most high.* And *salvation* could mean healing and health in the present world rather than deliverance from sin and eternal life.[48] So although the message *sounded true,* its *source* would have led to *confusion* in the minds of the hearers[49] who would associate the gospel with their own polytheistic beliefs.[50] This would lead people to turn to the serpent for damnation rather than to Christ for salvation.

In Acts 16, the author of confusion was confounded by the power of God's Word. Paul said to the spirit, "In the name of Jesus Christ I command you to come out of her" (Acts 16:18). Paul's exorcism of the spirit was part of his evangelistic work. When the spirit heard Paul speak in the name of Jesus, it left the girl immediately. By invoking Jesus' name, Paul pointed to the clear distinction between Christ and the spirit that controlled the girl. This set the record straight on the true source of salvation.

When the gospel is proclaimed it brings opposition to the forefront. In response to God's truth, Satan spins his lies, both publicly and privately, in the hearts and minds of the listeners. Those who bear witness to the gospel in the power of the Spirit have Christ's authority to overcome this spiritual opposition.[51] True salvation, including freedom from spiritual bondage, comes only through Jesus Christ.[52]

When the slave girl's owners realized their "hope of making money" through the girl's spiritual power was gone, they had Paul and Silas arrested, beaten and thrown into prison. Notice the close connection between demonic opposition and human opposition to the gospel. The girl's owners seemed only interested in money, but their greed allowed them to become pawns in the dragon's clutches to do his bidding.[53] The Roman jailer, as a result of his duty to carry out the will of the local officials, played a part in the binding of Paul and Silas as well. Each of these people, as a result of their position in the present world, became a tool Satan tried to use to arrest the advance of God's kingdom.

Ironically, Paul and Silas were the only people in the story who really were free. Even when they were bound in chains, they experienced freedom brought about by God's Spirit. In the darkest circumstances they were able to lift their voices in praise to God. About midnight a violent earthquake shook the prison, opening its doors and causing the prisoners' chains to fall off (Acts 16:25-26). God freed Paul and Silas so they could continue to preach the gospel.[54]

Brother Yun was imprisoned in a maximum security prison for preaching, training leaders and leading house churches in China. Yet on the morning of May 5, 1997, he walked out through normally locked iron doors, passed prison guards and crossed the prison courtyard. Yun literally walked out of the main gate of the prison to freedom. This was not because the officials had released him, but because God had provided the means of his escape.[55] The power of God's Word cannot be bound by human chains!

When the Philippian jailer burst into the room of Paul and Silas, he was considering suicide because he feared the prisoners' escape. When the guard saw that Paul and Silas were still there, he fell at their feet and cried out, "Sirs, what must I to be saved?" (Acts 16:30). This polytheistic jailer, who had no doubt heard about the slave girl and seen the power of the earthquake, may have mistaken them for gods.[56] Paul and Silas pointed him to the One who provides freedom from sin and eternal life: "Believe in the Lord Jesus, and you will be saved—you and your household" (Acts 16:31).

The jailer responded immediately. He washed Paul's and Silas's wounds (Acts 16:33). The jailer turned his attention from his own concerns to the needs of others. He not only experienced God's love, but also became a channel through which God's love flowed to others. Then the jailer and his family were baptized as a public confession of their faith in Christ.[57] The family ate a meal with the apostles, "filled with joy, because they [came] to believe in God" (Acts 16:34). It seems likely that this was both a fellowship meal and a celebration of the Lord's Supper[58] since it was a celebration of this family's newfound faith in Christ.[59]

Paul became distressed in Athens because the city was "full of idols" (Acts 17:16). A more literal translation here would be that Athens was "covered with idols" or "smothered with idols."[60] Descriptions of Athens at that time grab the imagination—a "forest of idols"; "there were more idols than people"; on some streets there were so many images that it was difficult for pedestrians to proceed; there were "more images in Athens than in the rest of Greece combined."[61] The Athenians believed this multitude of gods could provide them with healing, happiness, and pleasure, relief from anxiety, protection from fate, and life after death.[62]

Contemporary Western Christians sometimes disregard idolatry as superstition, assuming idols are powerless. But Paul assumed that "demonic spirits" were at work through idols (1 Cor. 10:20). These spirits may, for a time, provide healing, relief and protection for those who worship the idols in order to gain a foothold in the lives of the worshippers. Once this foothold is gained, the spirits are not easily vanquished, save through the power of Jesus Christ.

The Japanese are, for the most part, secular and hedonistic in their everyday lives. Most of their time is spent in pursuit of money, material possessions, worldly pleasure and personal satisfaction. Little regard is given to spiritual life, except on special occasions such as weddings, baby dedications, funerals, or building dedications. Aside from these occasions, once or twice a year most Japanese go to their local Shinto shrine or Buddhist temple to pray for protection and happiness. Although this contact with the spirit world through idolatry is extremely limited, it is enough to give these spirits a foothold in their lives. These spirits, whether in ancient Athens or contemporary Tokyo, produce "supernatural opposition" to the proclamation of the gospel.[63]

Those attempting to share the gospel in the post-Christian West run up against this wall as well when they meet people who discount the reality of the transcendent, see "finite reality" self-contained, and deny that there is any spiritual aspect of existence, human or otherwise.[64] The postmodern West has been blinded by demonic spirits at work through the idols of radical distrust of authority, moral and cultural relativism, and global economic expansionism.

We often find ourselves trying to explain the gospel to people whose initial question is, "What do you mean by the word 'god'?" When there is a myriad of so-called gods, it is easy for people to conclude that there is no real God at all. In this situation, speaking of a God who sent His Son comes across as nonsense. This is because people who are filled with doubt may believe in nothing.

We gain valuable insight from Paul's approach when he preached at the Areopagus. Paul wanted to help his audience recognize the reality of both God's existence and His saving action through Jesus Christ.[65] But he connected with his listeners on the basis of their own personal experience. Paul pointed to the Athenians spirituality displayed through their thousands of "objects of worship" (Acts 17:22, 23). Then Paul confirmed what the people already thought: that he had come to talk about an "unknown god" (Acts 17:23). This god, Paul said, was the Creator and rightful Ruler of all things (Acts 17:24), who made human beings (Acts 17:25) and determines the course of their lives (Acts 17:26). It is possible for us to have a relationship with this God because "he is not far from each one of us" (Acts 17:27). Their proper response should be to "repent" (Acts 17:30), to turn away from idols and serve the God who created and loves us. Each person will be judged by God on the basis of his or her decision to turn from idols and to follow the Jesus Christ (Acts 17:31).[66]

I was talking with a new Christian about how to witness. He said he found it difficult to explain Jesus to non-Christians without first explaining that God created them and cares for them. This is exactly what Paul did. The purpose of Paul's message was to open his listeners' spiritual eyes. He called them to live on the basis of this newfound spiritual truth: to change their spiritual loyalty from false gods to the one true God. While some rejected Paul's message, others who heard believed (Acts 17:38).

People will not trust in the Son until they experience the reality of His Father's love. This experience comes through personal recognition that God has provided for us through His work of creation, and that He continues to provide for us by interceding in our everyday lives.

When Paul began teaching in the synagogue in Ephesus, Jewish opposition caused him to relocate to the "lecture hall of Tyranus" where he continued to teach for over two years (Acts 19:8-10). As people passed through Ephesus, many heard the gospel, believed in Christ, stayed with Paul long enough to receive further instruction, and then carried back their faith with them to various points throughout the province.[67] This bought about remarkable results. "All of the Jews and Greeks who lived in the province of Asia heard the word of the Lord" (Acts 19:10).

As elsewhere, Paul's proclamation of gospel brought spiritual opposition. Seven sons of a local Jewish priest named Sceva tried to cast out evil spirits in Jesus' Name (Acts 19:13-14). This did not work, however, because Sceva's sons had "no direct connection with Jesus."[68] They were over-powered by the demon-possessed man (Acts 19:15-16) because they had no authority over the evil spirit that controlled him. In contrast, Paul's works of healing and exorcism authenticated the power of God's Word to overcome the evil in the present world (Acts 19:11-12).[69]

Satan's authority, displayed through disease and demonic possession, was overturned by the power God's Word.[70] This confirmed Paul's spiritual authority as a follower of Jesus Christ.[71] The use of Jesus' Name is only effective when it flows out of a personal relationship with the living Christ.[72] Many people in Ephesus turned away from their involvement in witchcraft and the occult to faith in Jesus Christ (Acts 19:17, 18).[73] The Ephesians realized that in comparison with the value of God's Word, their magical incantations and sorcery were worthless (Acts 19:19).[74]

Producing New Life

Our identification as Christians by others is a matter of both belief and behavior. Believing in Christ causes us to follow Him, and as we follow Him with become like Him, so that others come to see His character in us. Those who receive the Holy Spirit are transformed so that their lives bear witness for Christ before the world. It is those who receive the Spirit who have their sins forgiven (Acts 2:38) and are saved from the fallen condition of the present world (Acts 2:40). God's Spirit works to reproduce Jesus' character in them. This spiritual transformation is expressed through fellowship with other believers (Acts 2:42), service to others (Acts 2:43-45), and especially through bold witness for Jesus Christ.[75]

As a result of Peter's preaching on Pentecost, the people were "cut to the heart" (Acts 2:37). Peter's message about Jesus was the tool the Holy Spirit used to bring about conviction. The people were cut to the heart because of their rejection of Jesus Christ. They had not believed Jesus was God's Son, so they had crucified Him. God the Father confounded their rejection by raising Jesus from the dead. It was their recognition and confession of this sin, accompanied by repentance and faith, which brought salvation. The gospel is the Spirit's double-edged sword which cuts to the heart (Heb. 4:12), bringing about both repentance from sin and faith in Christ.[76]

When the gospel witness arrived in Antioch it was the third largest city in the Roman Empire, surpassed only by Rome and Alexandria.

In Antioch, two groups of evangelists divided the work in order to more effectively saturate the city with God's Word. The proclamation of the gospel extended beyond those with a Jewish ethnic and religious identity (Acts 11:19) to include those who identified more readily with the dominant Greek-speaking Gentile culture of the city (Acts 11:20). This included both Jewish proselytes[77] and Gentiles with no previous connection to Judaism who came to faith in Christ directly out of a polytheistic background.[78] "The Lord's hand was with them, and a great number of people believed and turned to the Lord" (Acts 11:21). The Holy Spirit used these witnesses to bring about repentance, faith in Christ and new life among those who heard their message.[79]

Faith in Christ and turning from the old way of life in order to follow Him are two sides of the same coin. A person cannot truly follow Jesus without first believing in Him. And when authentic faith is present, it is accompanied by a change in the way a person lives as he or she walks in obedience to Christ. This external change in lifestyle that accompanied their newfound faith in Christ caused the believers in Antioch to be labeled "Christians" for the first time (Acts 11:26).

Repentance and faith both are necessary for salvation. Through *repentance,* people turn away from their old way of life. This is not turning away from sin in general, but rather turning from the specific sin of rejecting Jesus.[80] It does not matter what other sins people turn away from if they continue to reject Christ. But when they give up their rejection of Jesus, they can begin to follow Him. *Faith* is essentially *trust in Christ*.

Trust in Christ leads to a commitment to "follow Him" (Luke 9:23), to walk as Jesus walked "in His steps" (1 Pet. 2:21). Repentance and faith mean to stop rejecting Jesus and to begin to follow Him.

In Acts 2, the people who turned to Christ did not only follow Him as individual believers. They formed a new community committed to study God's Word (Acts 2:42), care for one another (Acts 2:42, 44, 46), pray (Acts 2:42), worship (Acts 2:43, 47), and proclaim of the gospel through both word and deed (Acts 2:45-47).[81]

Real discipleship takes place as people share their lives together. When people become Jesus for one another, reflecting His characteristics of humility, gentleness, patience and love (Eph. 4:2), they encourage each other to do "works of service, so that the body of Christ may be built up" (Eph. 4:12). The goal of this life together in the Christian communities we call local churches is spiritual maturity, measured by our reflection of Christ's character (Eph. 4:13).

In these Christian communities, God's Word is the tool the Spirit uses to re-form believers so that they come to resemble Christ. Paul writes that it is "useful for teaching, rebuking, correcting and training in righteousness, so that the man of God may be equipped for every good work" (2 Tim. 3:16-17). As people are nourished through the study and application of God's Word, they become healthy, growing, productive Christians.[82] By living out Christ's teachings together, they urge one another on towards spiritual maturity.

The true measure of effectiveness in disciple-making is the number of growing Christians who are assimilated and participating in growing local churches. If we lead people to confess faith in Christ it is good. If we lead them to follow the Lord with the initial public confession of faith that is baptism, it is even better. But we must press on to involve people meaningfully in the Body of Christ. This is where the Holy Spirit does the real, long term work of character transformation. In this kind of church, "deep, quality relationships" nurture "spiritual growth." People experience spiritual healing and personal fulfillment as their lifestyles, values, actions and words come to reflect Jesus.[83]

Reaching the World by Changing Hearts

The story of the Christian mission is about the advance of the gospel, beginning at Jerusalem and extending to all nations of the world. Geographical expansion is possible because of the gospel's penetration into the hearts of individuals. This penetration takes place when people who hear the gospel are moved by the Holy Spirit to turn from sin, trust in Christ, and experience eternal transformation. Internal penetration and external expansion occur contemporaneously and co-dependently—each one is necessary for the other to take place.

A Japanese exchange student studying in California became involved with Christians through an international friendship group that met near his campus. He began to meet weekly with a student worker. At first the exchange student was only interested in learning English. But as he got to know the student worker, the Japanese student became interested in the Bible as well. Over time God's Word penetrated his heart. A short time before he returned to Japan, this exchange student committed his life to Christ and was baptized.

After he returned to Tokyo, the young man connected with a missionary and they began to meet two or three times a month to study God's Word, pray and discuss issues related to the young man's experience as a new Christian. The Japanese young man was very hesitant about what he should do. He only knew that he needed to grow as a Christian and that he wanted to serve God.

Through their times of study together, God's Word continued to penetrate the young man's heart. This brought about changes in thought, attitude and behavior. As the Japanese man came to understand more deeply Christ's love, his doubts and fears were turned to joy. Tentativeness was replaced by a desire to see his family and friends come to faith in Christ. He acted on this desire by trying to share his faith with people he knew. The young man developed a vision to open a coffee shop in a building his family owned in the heart of Tokyo. This coffee shop will be used to reach people for Christ through conversational English, music coffee houses, Bible study and worship.

There are still spiritual barriers to overcome. While the young man's eternal victory in Christ is secure, the daily spiritual battle rages on. The young man still has sinful habits to overcome. He struggles daily with consistency in his devotional life. He needs to become more assertive in sharing his faith. Family members and friends have proven to be resistant to the gospel, raising old doubts about his inadequacy as a Christian. There are temptations to participate in the ancestral rituals and idolatry that play an important part in Japanese culture. The Spirit continues to wield His sword, penetrating ever deeper into this Japanese man's heart. As the Spirit uses the Word to make this man more like Jesus, He also uses this man to bring his corner of the world to Christ.

Understanding and Applying God's Word

1. ***What were some results of the outpouring of the Holy Spirit on the Day of Pentecost?***
2. ***Should healing have any relationship to the proclamation of the gospel today?***
3. ***What evangelistic strategy is suggested by the story of Philip and the Ethiopian eunuch?***
4. ***Why is hearing an important aspect of evangelism?***
5. ***How does the Holy Spirit use the proclamation of God's Word to break down barriers that segregate people, such as ethnicity, language, culture and social class?***
6. ***What are some examples of our tendency to "Simonize" God's Spirit in evangelism and discipleship? How can we guard against this tendency?***

7. *How does Satan work through belief systems to prevent people from trusting in Christ?*
8. *Where should we begin when we are attempting to explain the truth to those who have false belief systems?*
9. *What is the goal of Christian community?*
10. *What is the measure of effective disciple-making?*

CHAPTER SIX

GROWING DISCIPLES IN THE BODY OF CHRIST

The growth of Christianity in Asia, Africa and Latin America in the last half century has been astonishing. When the Communists claimed control of China in 1949, there were no more that 2 million Christians; now that total is estimated at between 60 and 100 million. Similar growth has been seen in other Asian nations. In South Korea the number of believers has increased from 300,000 in 1920 to over 12 million today. In India there are thought to be as many as 62 million believers, and this number is expected to climb to over 100 million by 2025. Even in Vietnam there are over 9 million Catholics, and Protestants have increased to between 50,000 and 70,000 believers.[1]

In Africa, in 1950 only twenty-five percent of the population was Christian. By 2001, this figure had swelled to forty-eight percent. In many countries in sub-Saharan Africa, the figure is closer to sixty percent.[2] This amounts to almost 390 million Christians in Africa, and is expected to increase to 595 million by 2025.[3]

Roman Catholicism has been a part of Latin American culture since the sixteenth century. In the twentieth century, charismatic renewal breathed new life into Christianity in that part of the world. Since 1900, the evangelical movement has increased from one percent of the population to over twelve percent—from 700,000 people to over 55 million. Of that number, over 12 million belong to Pentecostal and Charismatic churches.[4] Many mainline Protestant and Roman Catholic churches are charismatic in their theology and practice as well.

With this explosive growth of Christianity in the two-thirds world, we might assume that we are succeeding at the task of making disciples. However, we need to remember that winning converts and making growing disciples of Jesus Christ is not necessarily the same thing. In the midst of immense numerical growth, there is the persistent concern that in too many places Christianity is "a mile wide and an inch deep." That is, Christianity has spread over a broad area, but in some cases it has not penetrated beneath the surface in order to transform the hearts and minds of the people. For example, much of the growth of Christianity in Africa has been among African Indigenous Churches, some of which have a tendency to blend Christianity with indigenous religious beliefs and practices. In the "Christianization" of Europe many animistic practices were "integrated into the church and never completely extinguished."[5] The current resurgence of witchcraft, the worship of earth goddesses, druidism and shamanism suggests not that Christianity in Europe is failing, but rather that in many cases Christianity in Europe has formed only a thin veneer covering a deeply entrenched "paganism."[6] Society in the United States is increasingly characterized as "post-Christian." For many people, a do-it-yourself "marketplace" approach to spirituality has become more common than a personal commitment to faith in Christ.[7] Even many who claim to be "Born-again Christians" have very little understanding of Christian doctrine and practice: one fourth believe in communication with the dead, one-third in reincarnation and astrology, and over half in psychic powers.[8]

When I lived in Kitakyushu in southwest Japan, missionaries and pastors moaned that too many of our people were spiritually immature. They would show up on Sunday to warm a pew, but then do nothing about their faith between Sundays. There was little understanding of the Bible, little prayer and little evangelism. We had too few pastors, too few laypeople trained to lead, and too few people to lead. The churches were dying.

When I moved to Tokyo, the situation looked a little different. There were more vibrant churches, and new churches were being planted every year. There also was church growth, particularly in international churches that were reaching young globalized Japanese who had come into contact with Christianity while they lived abroad and then returned home with a spiritual hunger to know more. But there also was much that was the same: effective Bible teaching, prayer and evangelism was limited to the few. Many churches had a shortage of trained leadership. And while some evangelism was taking place, ninety percent of the 35 million people in the Tokyo metropolitan area claimed they had never met a Christian, much less heard the gospel.

Then I came to Bolivar, Missouri, a small town in the Midwest United States. The setting certainly is different from Japan. For example, if the largest church in our community were moved to Japan it would be one of the five largest churches in that nation! On the other hand, about seventy percent of the people don't go to church anywhere. There are many lost people, and much work is left to be done in the task of making disciples, even in a small town in the Bible belt.I had the opportunity to talk with some committed Christians in Bolivar about what is needed to impact our town and the surrounding county for Christ. I heard about many of the same issues that we had in Kitakyushu and Tokyo: too little understanding of the Scriptures and even less application, too little prayer, and too little evangelism. In short, the primary problem with reaching our community is *inside* rather than *outside* the church. We will not be able to reach our community for Christ until believers get serious about following Christ.

Bill Easum sounds a wake-up call when he writes,

> It's time we called the decline of our churches what it is—a failure to grow strong Christians. Pastors [have] allowed people to vegetate, to become little more than pew potatoes. We've made domesticated house pets out of them and have refused to let them out of the sandbox. We've made their lives shallow and unproductive . . . Our churches are little more than hospices where people wait to die and hope to God

that the money doesn't run out before they do.[9]

While many people inside our churches understand very little about the faith they claim to believe in, those outside the church have drifted into a neo-pagan "designer faith" in which they develop their own personalized combination of deities: money, materialism, power, popularity, sex, leisure, happiness, astrology, Wicca, environmentalism, and so forth. As a result, when a Christian refers to "God," the non-Christian may honestly ask, "Which one?"[10] Unfortunately, in many cases the Christian's understanding may be so limited that he or she is unable to provide a satisfactory answer to this question which once seemed simple, but has become increasingly complex.

We need to develop churches that are authentic communities of committed followers of Jesus Christ. In these communities, believers invest their lives together in order to encourage one another to grow in relationship to Christ. In this context, a personal relationship with Jesus Christ becomes the hub of not only the community, but also of the entirety of each person's life.[11] Easum writes that people today are not interested in the "theological Christ." They are interested in the "personal Jesus" that has the power to change lives. They will only meet Him through the witness of those who have a daily, vital relationship with the living Christ.[12]

The study and application of God's Word is essential for the development of authentic Christian community. The message of Jesus

Christ provides for the inception, continuation and completion of the process of spiritual growth. Each stage finds its foundation in a trust relationship with Jesus Christ. Scripture provides the proper shape for a community that is centered in Christ. The goal is to develop an environment in which believers can grow to the point that their every thought, word and deed bring glory to the God who is at work in Christ and who continues Christ's work in us.

Word-Driven Training

In Paul's second letter to Timothy, he writes about two sources of "strength for the Christian pilgrimage": the example of other believers and instruction in the Scriptures.[13] Both of these factors have their greatest impact in faith communities where Christians teach, train and encourage one another to live in accordance with God's Word.

Timothy lived in a world, not so different from our own, where spiritual opposition made living a godly life difficult. Paul repeatedly encouraged him to "guard the good deposit [of faith] entrusted to [him]" (1:14), to "endure hardship like a good soldier of Christ Jesus" (2:3), and to "flee the evil desires of youth, and pursue righteousness, faith, love and peace" (2:22). The reason for these words of encouragement is that "there will be terrible times in the last days" (3:1). Paul reminds Timothy that Paul had endured imprisonment (1:8-9) and persecution (3:11) for the sake of Christ. In fact, Paul writes, "Everyone who wants to live a godly life in Christ Jesus *will be persecuted"* (2 Tim. 3:12, emphasis mine). That is to say, those who attempt to live in pursuit of becoming like Christ inevitably experience opposition.

It is not easy to put aside the things of the world in order to pursue the things of God. We suffer continual bombardment from the internet, television, magazines, books, email and cell-phone traffic, and even well-meaning friends, that promise us satisfaction if we will pursue our lust for the more and the better: more money so we can acquire better possessions; more gas mileage in better cars; more power and better influence; and more technology with better potential for communication. We pursue what we can control, rather than yielding to God because we do not want to yield to His control.

For spiritual growth to occur, Paul tells us we must "continue in what [we] have learned and have become convinced of" (3:14). This is an imperative statement: a command not merely to learn and develop convictions about the things of God, but to act on the basis of these convictions under the leadership of God's Spirit.

Genuine Christian communities encourage this type of action when believers hold one another accountable for both understanding and applying God's Word. In this setting, "healthy and productive" Christians receive preparation for both living in the world and serving in God's Kingdom.[14]

God's Word provides the basis for spiritual transformation. "All Scripture is God-breathed" (3:16). The Scriptures are the result of the activity of God's Spirit within individual writers so that the product is not merely a human work, but rather a display of God's "own life and character."[15] As a result, when we read or hear the Scriptures, we not only learn about God and His will. God actually meets us in His Word, confronts us with His holiness, convicts us of our sinfulness, and calls us to become more like Jesus. Donald Bloesch writes that this "conjunction between the Word of God and sacred Scripture [occurs] by the action of God's Spirit."[16] He "must break into our reasoning processes and remold them if we are ever to know him as he knows us."[17] Thomas D. Lea and Hayne P. Griffin write,

> Timothy's study of the Scriptures has grounded him in that wisdom and enlightenment that leads to faith in Jesus Christ. The Scriptures lead to salvation but only as they point to Christ. The Scriptures themselves do not provide salvation, but they do point to the Savior who can provide it.[18]

In 2 Timothy 3:15, the meaning of *salvation* is not limited to "conversion." Rather, salvation continues to impact the believer's life as he or she is transformed by God's Word.[19] This takes place by means of a four-fold process: "teaching, rebuking, correcting and training in righteousness" (3:16). The first two aspects have to do coming to understand spiritual truth: the Scriptures *teach* what is true and *rebuke* what is false. "The Holy Spirit brings to light where we have departed from the prescribed path of teaching" in order to help us return to the way of truth.[20] *Correction* and *training* are concerned with behavior. Correction shows us where we have done wrong, and training shows us how to do right.

The word *paideia,* translated "training," is the Greek word used for the "discipline" of children in order to bring about character development.[21] Hull notes that this must be a "gradual, ongoing process" that is "intentional and guided." When this kind of training is applied to spiritual development, it is only possible in the context of loving relationships in which believers hold one another "accountable" to act in obedience to God's Word. This does not occur when we only interact with people at a safe distance. Accountability necessitates "rolling up our sleeves" and "getting involved"[22] in the messy aspects of people's lives.

In the course of a semester, it is not unusual to have students come to me who are confused and depressed because of relational issues. These issues may be due to either mistakes they have made in dating or marriage, or abuse they have suffered at the hands of a parent or another trusted person. In these situations, without fail I have found the words of Scripture to be the greatest source of consolation, encouragement and instruction. But if these students only hear the words of Scripture and do nothing about what they hear, they do not experience lasting change in their lives. The key is to encourage them to move beyond only being "hearers of the Word" to also become "doers of the Word" (James 1:22). The best way I have found to do this is to share with them about the results of applying the words of Scripture to relationships and situations in my own life. This provides an example of what God's Word looks like when it takes on flesh in the life of the believer.

Timothy's was not a theoretical knowledge of the Scriptures based solely on his personal study of the text. Rather, Timothy had learned how the meaning of the Scriptures impacts life by observing the examples of his grandmother Lois and his mother Eunice (1:5). He also had seen Paul's "teaching, way of life, purpose, faith, patience, love, and endurance" (3:10). It was this fleshing out of biblical truth by other people in the context of significant relationships that helped Timothy to understand what it meant to follow Christ.

This biblical training produces Christians who are "thoroughly equipped for every good work" (3:17). Donald Guthrie writes that Scripture is a "God-given instrument designed to equip [the Christian] completely for his work."[23] We must be clear that the work God prepares us for is His work which He intends to do through us. The thorough application of Scripture in the life of believers prepares us to become His instruments that are wholly suited to carry out His purposes in the world. As God's Word drives the church in process of making disciples, "people are converted, the body grows, and God is glorified."[24]

Communities for Spiritual Growth

Spiritual growth takes place when we are encouraged to *live God's Word* in both the Christian community and the broader community which makes up our corner of the world. When God's Word is lived in Christian community the result is authentic *fellowship,* centered in the common purposes of love for God and love for one another (Luke 10:27).[25] When isolated individuals who hunger for meaningful relationships see Christians love one another in a sacrificial Christ-like manner, they are compelled to come to Him.[26] Bill Easum and Tom Bandy write,

> Faith development needs quality intimacy with people who share one's desire for God. Mutual support, honesty, respect and prayer help people find their way through ambiguity.[27]

In this context, God's Word cannot be taught in an obtuse, rationalistic manner. Rather, the Scriptures must be brought into the conversation with the concerns of everyday life. People must be able to see from the Scriptures what Christ-likeness should look like at home, the office, the mall and the ball park. And the fellowship of believers should be such that people are actually encouraged to allow God's Word to be fleshed out through them as they walk through the world.

Spiritual growth is most likely to occur in a *safe environment* in which people are free to be themselves and to openly discuss issues. Randy Frazee mentions five characteristics of Christian communities that foster this sense of spiritual openness.[28] First, participants are *spontaneous* in terms of when and where they meet, what they do together, and what they talk about. Rather than being fueled by the need for completion of a task, they are fueled by relationships. They live life together. Rather than meeting together at 9:30

a.m. every Sunday for one hour, they may meet any day of the week (or everyday for that matter) at places of mutual convenience to deal with the issues of life. I know of Christians who meet together in homes, coffee shops, restaurants, karaoke bars, hospital community rooms and parks on various days and at various times, from early in the morning to late at night, because these places and times meet the needs of those who are meeting together. This sense of spontaneity does not mean there is a lack purpose; rather the purpose of becoming like Christ is brought into every conversation and activity together.

Second, believers are *available* to provide a listening ear, to lend a helping hand, or to just hang out. In the rapid pace of contemporary society in which people rush from one appointment to another, learning to slow down long enough to make ourselves available is counter-cultural. My wife and I have found that sometimes we must plan one to three months ahead in order to enjoy a "spontaneous" evening of fellowship with close friends. And then in many cases our time together are interrupted by a business call. I have concluded that availability to God and others is a matter of spiritual discipline: it necessitates shutting out the noise of the outside world so that we can interact on a deep enough level to develop significant relationships.

Third, believers develop real community through *frequent interaction*. It is not enough to meet together once a month or even once a week. Taking their cue from the early church which met together daily (Acts 2:46), they maintain constant contact in order to encourage one another. While Christians in tribal societies might accomplish this by working in the fields together and gathering each evening in their village for a common meal, in fast-paced urban societies frequent interaction is likely to take place through communication technologies such as cell phone, email and text-messaging.

Fourth, safe environments tend to form when people take time to eat *common meals* together. This is a real challenge in a culture where families struggle to eat together more than a couple of times a week. But sharing a meal together has the unique power to bond people together into community and family. I have noticed that small groups that take time to eat together often become more open to sharing other aspects of their lives: their victories and defeats; their successes and sufferings.

A final characteristic of safe environments is a shared sense of *geography*. People who live in close proximity to one another are more easily available to see and interact with one another on a regular basis. People who live in the same community share common issues that they need to solve together. This sense of shared community is easy to achieve in a rural area or small town, but becomes more difficult in the city or suburbs. In this case, churches need to find ways to encourage believers that live in the same areas to interact and work together. This is best accomplished through geographically defined small groups or ministry action teams.

Spiritual growth also is encouraged through *mentoring relationships* in which "one person empowers another by sharing God-given resources," including "wisdom, experiences, patterns, habits of obedience, and principles."[29] A mentoring relationship begins when a potential mentor and a potential mentoree are "attracted" to one another. The mentoree may see value in the mentor's training, ability, experience, knowledge or influence, while the mentor is attracted by the mentoree's openness and willingness to learn. When the mentoree responds that he or she is willing to learn from the mentor, a relationship can be formed based on mutual accountability.[30]

I have noticed that a number of well meaning churches develop mentoring programs that vary in length from six weeks to three years. The problem with this kind of approach is that the goal of mentoring, like that of discipleship as a whole, is *relational*. It extends beyond the mentoring relationship to the personal relationship which they share in common with Jesus Christ. The goal of spiritual mentoring is getting to know and learning to follow Jesus.[31] The mentoring process that results in spiritual maturity is not a six week sprint, or even a three year run. It is more like a sixty year marathon! This is why the writer of Hebrews instructs us to "run *with perseverance* the race marked out for us" (12:1, emphasis mine). Paul Stanley and Robert Clinton write that those who finish this race well remain focused, experience continual intimacy with Christ, maintain discipline in their lifestyles and devotional lives, are lifetime learners, and have a network of meaningful, supportive relationships.[32]

There are so many potential obstacles to the mentoring process—everything from busy lifestyles to misplaced priorities. Even legitimate concerns such as illness, economic factors and family issues can get in the way of mentoring one another towards spiritual maturity. If we are going to have any hope of success, churches and individual believers will have to give mentoring a high priority. Like athletes preparing for the Olympics, they will have to "throw off everything that hinders and the sin that so easily entangles" in order to "run the race" (Heb. 12:1).

What typically happens is that we make a list of the obstacles that might prevent us from completing the race. Then we convince ourselves that given all the other things we have going in our busy lives, forming a mentoring relationship in which we can encourage and be encouraged in the process of spiritual growth really is not very practical. So before we even place our feet in the starting blocks we throw in the towel and walk off the track! What we fail to realize is the Christian race is a team sport. The obstacles that we could never overcome by ourselves can be conquered when Christians work together under the leadership of the Holy Spirit.

One advantage to attending Baylor University was learning to "Bear" with the struggles of a private university trying to compete in athletics against some of the largest state universities in the United States. During my sophomore year our football team, which was having a dismal season, prepared to host the University of Arkansas for our homecoming game. The Razorbacks came into the game boasting an 8-0 record, ranked fifth in the nation. The Bears had won only two games and no one expected us to be able to stay on the field with Arkansas. However, Baylor pulled out a stunning 24-17 upset. As I look back on that game played over twenty-five years ago, I realize no individual player could take credit for our victory over the Hogs that day; it was a team effort.

In much the same way, solitary Christians cannot achieve spiritual victory alone. Churches must develop the kind of environment in which Christians will have a sense of teamwork, holding one another accountable to grow to maturity in Christ. They must encourage one another to take obedience to God's Word seriously, and model for one another what obedience looks like. Finally, they must stand together against the assault of Satan and the problem of sin in order to experience victory in serving Christ. What none of us can achieve alone can be accomplished together in the power of the Holy Spirit.

The Power of Mutual Confession

Spiritual growth takes place in churches that encourage the *confession of sin.* The Greek word for confession, *homologeo,* literally means "to say the same thing." This means that we agree with God to call sin what He calls sin. Not only that, we take full responsibility for our sinful acts, agreeing with God that we deserve judgment and stand in need of His cleansing.[33] Confession is counter-intuitive because of our human tendency to deny we have done anything wrong. My experience is that people, both Christians and non-Christians, do not want to admit their faults. The words, "I'm sorry, I was wrong," get caught in our hearts and never come out of our mouths. Yet confession of sin is necessary if we are going to enjoy the fullness of our relationship with God and others. John writes,

> If we claim to have fellowship with [God] yet walk in darkness, we lie and do not live by the truth. But if we walk in the light, as he is in the light, we have fellowship with one another, and the blood of Jesus, his Son, purifies us from all unrighteousness. If we claim to be without sin, we deceive ourselves and the truth is not in us. If we confess our sins, he is faithful and just and will forgive our sins and purify us from all unrighteousness (1 John 1:6-9).

It is clear from the context that "fellowship with one another" refers not to fellowship among Christians, but rather to our fellowship with God. This only takes place when there is a "confession of definite sins" accompanied by a "determination to avoid sin."[34] When true confession takes place there is a turning from sin and accompanied by a heart-felt desire to live more fully in obedience to Christ.

Because of our human tendency to cover over our sins, we must not only encourage the confession of sins to God. We must also develop an environment in which believers feel at ease to confess their sins to one another. James writes, "Confess your sins to each other and pray for each other, so that you may be healed. The prayer of a righteous man is powerful and effective" (5:16). This is an aspect of the priesthood of the believer (1 Pet. 2:5) that we provide for one another as part of the Body of Christ, hearing one another's confession, praying for each other, and reminding each other that in Christ there is forgiveness of sin and new life. In this way, we act on the authority Christ has given to His followers to participate in His work of forgiving sin (John 20:23).[35] In doing so, we relieve one another of the "burden of unconfessed sin" while also encouraging each other to "avoid sin" in the future. As members of the Body of Christ experience this forgiveness and encouragement, the church experiences spiritual purification which enables both the whole church and each member to more fully resemble Christ.[36]

This does not mean that Christians should make a general practice of confessing our sins before the whole church. There may be rare occasions when such general confessions of sin are necessary, such as when the sin of a key leader impacts the whole community. The church is made up of believers at various levels of spiritual maturity, and it is unwise to lay all our faults before those that are either unwilling or incapable of assisting us. Also, there may be those struggling with the issue of a loose tongue that are unable to resist the temptation to talk about others in a damaging way. Confession of sin places us in a vulnerable position, so we should only share "our deepest weaknesses and failures" with "trusted others."[37] For most people, that will mean of support group made up of two or three trusted friends in which mutual confession, prayer and encouragement can take place. Many times, this will be a part of a mentoring relationship, although there will be occasions when people need a support group made up of trusted peers apart from any other mentoring relationship they may participate in.

A Witnessing Community

A community of faith that has been transformed by God's Word bears witness to the truth of that Word in the world. Howard Snyder reminds us that while "evangelism is the first priority of the Church's ministry in the world," evangelism without personal transformation is impossible because "changed persons are necessary to change society."[38] We bear witness through both "verbal proclamation" and "demonstration of the good news." The truth of this message is most clearly seen when God's people live out what it means to be Christian community in the world.[39]

Michael Frost and Alan Hirsch write about *Elevation,* a café where people from a variety of backgrounds come together to participate in "art classes, philosophy discussion groups, film reviews, mural projects, dance classes, cooking classes," and other activities. The purpose is to allow "space" for Christians and non-Christians to talk about God, the meaning of life, and other key spiritual issues in a purposeful non-threatening manner.[40] Such an approach has great promise because it gives Christians the opportunity to enter into dialogue with non-Christians about essential issues related to faith and life on the non-Christians' turf.

There is no magic formula that dictates how this should look in every situation. There are, however, some key questions that can point us in the right direction. When we are trying to break down the wall that too often separates the church from the wider community, we must ask, "*Where* do people in this community gather?" And "*What kinds of activities* do they gather around?" In small towns across America's South and Midwest, women gather to make scrapbooks and quilts. So these are appropriate activities to use from disciple-making in these settings. But quilting would not work to reach the women in the slums of New Delhi. To reach them, local Christians must ask, "When, where and for what purpose do these women meet so that we can we can meet with them to share and live out the God's Word?"

I grew up in small town in Texas where local farmers gathered at a local café each morning to drink coffee and share stories. I have found this to be nearly a cultural universal in the South. When I drive through a small town in the morning I almost always find a café surrounded by trucks. So if the farmers gather at the café, we need to be there talking with them about what God's Word tells us about farming (which is a lot) and how they ought to live (which is even more).

The purpose of our witness to God's Word always will be to call people to an obedient relationship with Jesus Christ. But the manner of our witness will vary with the context. At times, there is much in the local society that is congruent with the teachings of God's Word that we can affirm. But in other cases, the local culture is morally and spiritually depraved so that we must bring a message of spiritual light into a setting darkened by sin. Usually there will be a mixture of good and bad, so that we must pray for discernment to know how to affirm what is right while redeeming what is wrong.[41]

Many Japanese people have incredible affection and respect for nature, but they may also deify nature, worshiping the gods of mountains, rivers, and forests. On the one hand, I can affirm the Japanese love for nature, but on the other hand I must encourage them to look beyond creation to have awe and respect for the Creator of all things.

Small Groups: Where Spiritual Growth Takes Place

My involvement in Christian small groups began when my parents enrolled me in the nursery at church when I was a few weeks old. Since that time, I have continually participated in small groups in a number of settings, from Sunday school classes that met in church buildings, to cell groups and house churches that met in homes, to accountability groups that met in restaurants and coffee shops. I have found that all of these forms of small groups have the *potential* to encourage spiritual growth, so I choose to paddle against the current that advocates only one type of small group as the *best* structure for spiritual growth.

Not every form of small group is equally effective in every setting. Some house churches are effective in countries where Christians must operate beneath the surface of visibility, and some are effective among population segments in other countries that prefer a looser form of organization. But not every house church in these settings is equally effective. House churches fail everyday. On the other end of the spectrum, some traditional churches that use Sunday school as their small group structure continue to flourish in small towns in the southern and mid-western United States, but many other traditional churches are dying. Also, there are some settings where neither a house church nor a traditional church is effective. For example, in tribal societies it is common to have a village church made up of practically every person in the village. This does not meet the standard definition of house church because it involves the whole community, and it does not fit the traditional church structure because there in no age-graded Sunday school. Still, small group life occurs as Christians gather, often informally, to study the Word and discuss how it applies to their lives.

What is most effective varies with the location and people we are working with. Take, for example, the case of young adults. I have found that many young adults enjoy meeting together in homes where they can relax and converse naturally. However, in Tokyo most young adults live in apartments that are so small that it would be difficult for more than four or five people to meet together. Moreover, young adults in Tokyo generally do not entertain in their homes. They are much more comfortable gathering in a restaurant or karaoke bar.

In Bolivar young married couples enjoy meeting in homes, but they do not like to meet together without someone to watch their children. So they have made compromises: either they meet at the church building with someone to watch the nursery, or they have the husbands and wives meet together on alternative nights with the other spouse left home to take care of the kids.

Rather than focus on only one type of small group as the ideal structure for every setting, I believe it is more helpful to consider a number of factors that can enable small groups to become more effective in encouraging spiritual growth. These factors apply equally, whether they are applied to traditional Sunday school classes, home groups, coffee shop gatherings, or house churches.

First, small groups are most effective in encouraging spiritual growth when they promote *active involvement.* This begins with discussion-oriented inductive Bible studies that encourage every person to share what God is showing them through His Word. Sharing takes place in both word and action. Believers not only talk about what transformed lives should look like; they actually encourage one another to live as those who have been transformed by the power of the gospel! Every person takes an active part in prayer (both in sharing requests and interceding for the needs of others), worship, fellowship, and service to those both inside and outside the group. The goal that drives all this activity is to embody the meaning the gospel, not only as individuals but also as a group. This means that some activities will be laid aside, or at least given less priority, because they do not convey the message of Christ. The group might take in a ball game or movie together on occasion as a means of fellowship, but they will not be driven by sports or entertainment. They will find their unity and direction in the mutual relationship they all share with Jesus Christ.

Second, spiritual growth is most likely when *close relationships* are formed for fellowship, encouragement, accountability and confession. Most people are only capable of maintaining between three and five close friendships. The kind of sharing, praying and encouraging that leads to this type of spiritual intimacy is more likely in small groups. But a small group structure does not automatically result in close relationships. There must be mutual trust, a willingness to be vulnerable, and a desire for cohesion before intimacy can occur. So what a small group *does* when they are together is extremely important. Just reading the Bible and filling in a worksheet together will not get it done. There must be shared life: time spent together in formal and informal settings, worshiping and studying God's Word together, serving together, eating and playing together, meeting one another's needs. Because of this, eating a meal together may be just as essential to the spiritual well-being of group members as studying God's Word together, when eating the meal is *recognized* as a means to apply God's Word in the context of community.

Third, small groups encourage spiritual growth when they allow every believer to serve on the basis of his or her *spiritual gifts*. Snyder notes that spiritual gifts are given to individual believers for the "body life" of the whole community.[42] There are some that view spiritual gifts as a means of personal control and self-aggrandizement. Nothing could be further from the truth. The word *charismata,* translated "spiritual gifts," is a derivative of the Greek word *charis,* meaning "grace." In other words, spiritual gifts are actually manifestations of God's grace through individuals within the Body of Christ. Every believer has at least one spiritual gift, but no believer has all of them. To say we "possess" the gifts may be saying too much. They are the Spirit's gifts which He uses through us to bring about Christ's glory by means of His Body at work in the world. The controlling principle behind the use of these gifts is that "to each one the manifestation of the Spirit is given for the common good" (1 Cor. 12:7). Individual members rightly use their gifts when they appropriate them for the benefit of others.[43]

When small groups are in proper balance, they allow the possibility for every believer to take the lead in his or her area of giftedness. Not only is the teacher essential, but so also is the evangelist, the prayer warrior, and the one gifted in the area of hospitality, the encourager and the servant. The person with the gift of service may be the most important leader of all, for it is this person that most clearly keeps before the group what it means to follow Christ. The teacher talks about the principles of Christ-like service, but it is the servant that leads by the example of serving others.

Fourth, small groups lead to spiritual growth when they empower believers to *penetrate the wider community* with the gospel of Jesus Christ. Gospel witness is both individual and corporate, and involves both words and actions. Small groups are most effective when participants work together to take the gospel into the streets, shops and homes of surrounding communities. I am not talking primarily about going out together on Saturday morning to knock on doors and hand out tracts, although there may be occasions when that is exactly what needs to be done. I have in mind taking Christian community into the wider community, portraying the love of Christ and the reconciling power of the gospel through actions and words so that those who do not believe in Christ will be drawn to Him.

Imagine a group of Christian men going to an older neighborhood of well-worn houses and doing repairs for senior adults that are physically and financially unable to do the repairs themselves. When people ask, "Why are you doing this?" the men answer, "Because Jesus loves you and we love you." The story of this example of Christ's love in action spreads throughout the community so that before long neighbors, friends and family members of the senior adults begin saying, "There is something different about these men; we want what they have." Home meetings are formed, the gospel is shared, and new lives are born into the kingdom. The number of believers in home groups multiplies to the point that a core group for a new church is formed. God's Word penetrates a community and new disciples are made. Through continued mentoring, they begin the process of growth towards spiritual maturity.

There are a number of factors that prevent small groups from becoming effective vehicles for spiritual transformation.

- *The focus of a group may turn inward* so that participants lose their vision for both the larger Body of Christ and the needs of a lost world. This often occurs because group members invest so much time and energy in one another's lives that they feel they have nothing left to invest in others. Anytime a group member says, "We enjoy each other, and can't really deal with new people coming in," there is a spiritual problem that must be resolved as soon as possible. Two ways to address this issue are for a small group to have ongoing ministry to those outside the group and to work on maintaining a spirit of hospitality to new people coming into the group.
- *A group may fail to study and apply God's Word*. When this occurs spiritual growth stops. In order to prevent this, a regular pattern of inductive Bible study in which members hold one another accountable for the application of God's Word must take place. In some cases, it is beneficial to form subgroups of two to three people who can hold each other accountable for application of God's Word. One useful model for these subgroups is *Life Transformation Groups* that meet weekly to hold each other accountable for personal Bible study and spiritual growth.[44]

- *They may become elitists,* believing they are spiritually superior to others. When this occurs there is a need for a dose of humility. Sometimes this can be administered by a visiting teacher or mentor working with the group for a short period of time, but in many cases humility will only be restored through the intervention of the Holy Spirit. This often occurs when one or more members of the group are placed in a position in which they are stretched beyond the limits of their own adequacy so they learn once again their need for dependence on God and that God's "power is made perfect in [our] weakness" (2 Cor. 12:9).
- *They may become only a recreation group,* dedicated primarily to pleasure rather than to spiritual growth. This is one reason it is essential for a small group to be part of a larger web for accountability, either as the cell of a larger congregation or as part of a network of house churches. When a small group is part of a larger body of believers, there is someone on the outside to help the small group remain focused on becoming obedient followers of Jesus Christ.
- *They may become only a work group* that wears people out rather than building them up. While ministry is essential to spiritual development, service without worship, prayer and Bible study is like running a marathon on an empty stomach: people will fall by the wayside rather

than continuing on in the process of spiritual growth. Small groups must strive to develop a balanced life that includes worship, study, prayer, and fellowship as well as service.

- *A group may become isolated from the larger Body of Christ*. When this happens, the full range of spiritual gifts needed to foster balanced growth is usually lacking. Howard Snyder writes about the need to maintain a "harmonious small-group/large-group rhythm," in which the small group provides the depth and the large group the breadth needed for balanced spiritual growth.[45] When small groups work together in coordinated fashion, they can provide "mutual support and encouragement" for each other as the Body of Christ supplies the spiritual gifts that are lacking in each individual group.[46]

Small groups provide the best opportunity for growth: spiritual growth of believers, numerical growth through evangelism and service, and reproductive growth through the formation of new small groups and churches. As individual believers mature in faith and bear witness to Christ's love in the community, new believers are added. When groups become too large, they multiply to form new groups, which may in turn lead to starting new churches.

Ed Stetzer points out that postmoderns who are searching for meaningful relationships often experience "conversion to the community" before they experience a "conversion to Christ." First they are drawn into a community of mutual love and concern which is the

Christian small group. It is here, "in conversation with Christian friends," that they come face to face with the One who is the source of this love, and they place their faith in Him.[47] This is only possible when small groups maintain an external focus on the needs of a fallen world coupled with a spiritual focus on the need of every person for a personal relationship with Jesus Christ.

The Greatest Challenge

In the early years of my ministry, I believed that knowledge would bring spiritual change: people only needed to have a clear understanding of God's Word for their lives to be changed. Now I know that unless people *decide* to act of what they know, spiritual change will not occur. In my book, *Hearing Christ's Voice*, I wrote,

> The reason so many seekers turn away from Christ is that they begin to understand Who Jesus really is and decide He is not what they really want. They decide they do not want the new life Jesus offers if this means following Him through the way of the cross (Luke 9:23). So they reject the way of life that Jesus offers to continue living their own way in a fallen world.[48]

When I lived in Kitakyushu, I participated in a small group for about ten years. Sometimes I led the group. At other times I mentored those that led the group. At still other times, I was simply a participant. Over time, this group developed incredible worship, intense intercessory prayer, and wonderful in-depth Bible study. Through this small group, many college students and young adults were taken to a new level of spirituality. Some grew in their relationship with Jesus Christ. Others came to trust in Jesus Christ for their salvation. Unfortunately, still others that had the opportunity to make life-changing decisions turned and walked away.

In particular, I remember one young woman that was my wife's student at Seinan Jo Gakuin College. She participated in our small group for two years. Whenever the group met, she was there singing, praying, interacting, and studying God's Word. On many occasions, my wife and I talked with her about her understanding of the gospel. From our conversations, it was clear that this young woman understood the message, but she was never willing to act on what she knew to place her faith in Christ. A short time after college graduation, she quit participating in the small group. We were heart-broken later when we heard that after college she lived with a series of young men out of wedlock, seeking the fulfillment in those relationships that she could have found in Christ.

This issue of the will does not end when people place their faith Christ. Many who call Jesus, "Lord," choose not to obey Him. Even those who claim to believe the Bible is God's Word often have a "take it or leave it" attitude when it comes to application. I have seen this on many occasions when leading Bible studies. At the end of the study someone will invariably say, "We understand you are saying, but . . ." and proceed to give me the reasons why they cannot do what the Bible says. Then they continue to live boring, stale, untransformed lives. They want God to do something for them, but they want Him to do it on their terms. They never catch on to the simple fact that experiencing God's power is dependent upon doing His will. God can change us, but He does this on the basis of the principles of His Word.

Spiritual change occurs when people grow tired of the status quo and begin to act on the basis of God's Word. At first they will experience resistance and ridicule, from Satan, the world, and many times even within the church. But as they persist in their diligence, empowered by the Holy Spirit, spiritual transformation comes. Eventually the spark kindled in a small corner grows into a raging flame until it envelops the whole community.

Understanding and Applying God's Word

1. ***How does our emphasis on numerical and/or spiritual growth relate to our understanding of making disciples?***
2. ***What is the relationship between the study of God's Word and the example of believers in the disciple-making process?***
3. ***What are some characteristics of churches that encourage spiritual growth?***
4. ***What is the place of confession in the disciple-making process?***
5. ***How can small groups encourage or limit spiritual growth?***
6. ***What is the greatest challenge in the process of making disciples? How can we deal with this challenge effectively?***

EPILOGUE

THE MEASURE OF LOVING GOD AND LOVING OTHERS

The heart of Old Testament faith is found in the *Shema,* Moses' injunction, "Hear, O Israel: The Lord our God, the Lord is one." There is only one true God, and we are commanded to "love the Lord your God with all your heart and with all your soul and with all your strength" (Deut. 6:4-5).

When asked which of the commandments is the greatest, Jesus replied that this command to love God with our whole being, coupled with the command to "love your neighbor as you love yourself" (Lev. 19:18) are the most important: "There is no commandment greater than these" (Mk. 12:29-31). Love for God and love for others are inextricably intertwined: we cannot have one without the other.

Israel was to bear witness to God's love for them and their love for God. God's love for them was evident in His gifts of freedom from bondage, a land of abundance, long life and national greatness. Israel also must make their love for God evident: they must speak of Him constantly "at home" and "along the road," when they "lie down" at night and when they "get up" in the morning (Deut. 6:7). Their love for God must be the controlling factor in their thoughts and deeds (Deut. 6:8) so that their homes would perpetuate love for God (Deut. 6:9).

The measure of Israel's love for God was the extent they "impressed" this passion to love Him upon their children, so that the following generations would become people that loved God as well. Unfortunately, Israel fell far short of this high standard. Rather than love for God, they perpetuated love for idols and empty religious rituals that resulted in a spiritual vacuum. Then they attempted to fill this vacuum with immorality borrowed from the neighboring Canaanites and political aspirations that led to court intrigue, a rapid succession of wicked rulers, and the eventual downfall of their nation.

We can learn a valuable lesson from the people of Israel. What we hold to be most important will be what we ultimately pass on to future generations. There are many good values—social justice, caring for the needs of others, starting and growing churches, Christian standards of morality and ethics—that are worthy of being passed on. All of these values should grow out of our ultimate desire to love God with all our heart, soul and strength. This is what each person must do, and what he or she must instill in others to do as well. Loving God and teaching others to love God is the essence of a life transformed through the work of Jesus Christ. And it is the reason God's Spirit uses His Word as His sword to cut away the unworthy dross from our lives so that Christ's glory may be seen in us.

Our spiritual maturity can be measured through the values of our descendants. Do our children and those we have the opportunity to influence love God and desire to live in obedience to His Word? Or are they shaped by the values of a culture which says a person is measured by his profession, the house she lives in, the car he drives, and the reputation of her friends? If those in our sphere of influence do not measure up to Jesus' standard of love for God and love for others, what are we doing about it?

I often ask, "If our Lord delays His coming until I go to be with Him, what kind of legacy will I leave behind?" If people only say, "He wrote good books," which is not likely, that will not count for much. If they say, "He was good teacher," that will have little lasting value. Even if they say, "He was a good husband and father," that is high praise, but it still won't account for much in the light of eternity. But if they say, "Through the example of his life, we learned what it means to love God and to follow Christ," there is no higher honor.

NOTES

Prologue

[1] Boyd Hunt, *Redeemed! Eschatological Redemption and the Kingdom of God* (Nashville: Broadman and Holman, 1993), 116.
[2] Clinton Arnold, *Powers of Darkness: Principalities and Powers in Paul's Letters* (Downers Grove, IL: InterVarsity, 1992), 153.
[3] Idem, *Three Crucial Questions about Spiritual Warfare* (Grand Rapids: Baker, 1997), 37-38.
[4] John H. Armstrong, "How Shall We Wage Our Warfare?" in *The Coming Evangelical Crisis,* ed. John H. Armstrong (Moody, 1996), 237.
[5] Robert Lightner, *Angels, Satan and Demons* (Nashville: Word, 1998), 159.
[6] Bryan G. Zacharias, *The Embattled Christian: William Gurnall and the Puritan View of Spiritual Warfare* (Carlisle, PA: Banner of Truth, 1995), 89-92.
[7] Neil T. Anderson, *The Bondage Breaker* (Eugene, OR: Harvest House, 1993), 83.
[8] Richard Alleine, *The World Conquered by the Faithful Christian,* reprint (Morgan, PA: Soli Deo Gloria, 1995), 6.
[9] Zacharias, 100; Alleine, 7.

Chapter One

[1] Barnabas Lindars, *The Gospel of John. New Century Bible Commentary,* Ronald E.Clements and Matthew Black, eds., (Grand Rapids: Eerdmans, 1972), 90.
[2] Frederic Louis Godet, *Commentary on John's Gospel* (Grand Rapids: Kregel, 1978), 262.
[3] Kelly Malone, *Hearing Christ's Voice: Living and Proclaiming the Gospel in an Embattled World* (Garland, TX: Hannibal, 2006), 29.
[4] Leon Morris, *The Gospel according to John. The New International Commentary on the New Testament,* F. F. Bruce, ed., (Grand Rapids: Eerdmans, 1971), 96-97.
[5] Gregory A. Boyd, *God at War: The Bible & Spiritual Conflict* (Downers Grove, IL: InterVarsity, 1997), 181.
[6] Stephen F. Noll, *Angels of Light, Powers of Darkness: Thinking Biblically about Angels, Satan & Principalities* (Downers Grove, IL: InterVarsity, 1998), 63, 69.

[7] Boyd, 157-64, takes the position that while Isa. 14:1-23 and Ezek. 28 refer, respectively, to the kings of Babylon and Tyre, they also "illumine the story of the rebellious king of the whole world."
[8] Noll, 33, 47.
[9] Gregory A. Boyd, *Satan and the Problem of Evil: Constructing a Trinitarian Warfare Theodicy* (Downers Grove, IL: InterVarsity, 2001), 172.
[10] Boyd, *God at War,* 164, 165.
[11] Noll, 99, 101.
[12] Merrill F. Unger, *Biblical Demonology: A Study of Spiritual Forces at Work Today* (Grand Rapids: Kregel, 1994),
[13] Noll, 102.
[14] Lightner, 78.
[15] Boyd, *Satan and the Problem of Evil,* 301-02.
[16] Arnold, *Three Crucial Questions,* 75-76, mentions three contemporary approaches to dealing with the phenomenon of demonic possession described in the New Testament: demythologization, reinterpretation in terms of a naturalistic worldview (often psychologically), or take it at face value. The third approach, followed by most evangelical Christians, is the one adopted here.
[17]Sydney H. T. Page, *Powers of Evil: A Biblical Study of Satan and Demons* (Grand Rapids: Baker, 1995), 100-01.
[18] Ibid., 103-04.
[19] Ibid., 105-06; Robert C. Tannehill, *Luke* (Nashville: Abingdon, 1995), 193-94.
[20]R. C. H. Lenski, *Matthew* (Grand Rapids: Baker, 1973), 221-36.
[21] William Hendriksen, *Luke* (Grand Rapids: Baker, 1978), 621-22; Susan R. Garrett, *The Demise of the Devil* (Minneapolis: Fortress, 1989), 45-46; David Powlinson, *Power Encounters* (Grand Rapids: Baker, 1995), 129-30.
[22] Arnold, *Three Crucial Questions,* 81.
[23] S. Mark Heim, *Is Christ the Only Way: Christian Faith in a Pluralistic World* (Valley Forge, PA: Judson, 1985), 8.
[24] Ibid., 51-66, points out the tendency to bring Jesus down to size results in one who is too small to be the Savior of all human beings.
[25] Arnold, *Three Crucial Questions,* 56-60.
[26] Ibid., 66-68.
[27] Neil Anderson, *Victory over the Darkness: Realizing the Power of Your Identity in Christ* (Ventura, CA: Regal, 1990), 170.
[28] Philip Johnson, *The Wedge of Truth: Splitting the Foundations of Naturalism* (Downers Grove, IL: InterVarsity, 2000), 158.
[29] Garrett, 37.
[30] Lightner, 107.
[31] Kay Arthur, *Lord, Is It Warfare? Teach Me to Stand* (Sisters, OR: Multnomah, 1991), 180.
[32] Noll, 105.
[33] Arnold, *Three Crucial Questions,* 152.
[34] Ibid., 157-59.

[35] Charles A. Kimball, *Jesus' Exposition of the Old Testament in Luke's Gospel* (Sheffield, England: JSOT, 1994), 88-95.
[36] Timothy M. Warner, *Spiritual Warfare: Victory over the Powers of This Dark World* (Wheaton: Crossway, 1991), 75, 76.
[37] Tom Wright, *Bringing the Church to the World: Renewing the Church to Confront Paganism Entrenched in Western Culture* (Minneapolis: Bethany House, 1992), 100, 101.
[38] Donald G. Bloesch, *Jesus Christ: Savior and Lord* (Downers Grove, IL: InterVarsity, 1997), 143.
[39] Hunt, 10.
[40] Patrick Cate, "The Uniqueness of Christ and Missions," in *The Centrality of Christ in Contemporary Missions,* ed. Mike Barnett and Michael Pocock, Evangelical Missiological Society Series (Pasadena: William Carey Library, 2005), 47.
[41] Michael Green, *Evangelism in the Early Church,* revised ed. (Grand Rapids: Eerdmans, 2003), 22.

Chapter Two

[1] Douglas Groothius, *Truth Decay: Defending Christianity against the Challenges of Postmodernism* (Downers Grove, IL: InterVarsity, 2000), 22.
[2] R. R. Reno, "Postmodern Irony and Petronian Humanism: The New Challenges of Evangelism," in *The Strange New Word of the Gospel: Re-Evangelizing in the Postmodern World,* ed. Carl E. Braatan and Robert W. Jansen (Grand Rapids: Eerdmans, 2002), 65.
[3] Bill Easum, *Leadership on the Other Side: No Rules, Just Clues* (Nashville: Abingdon, 2000), 72, 73.
[4] Vinoth Ramachandra, *Gods that Fail: Modern Idolatry and Christian Mission* (Downers Grove, IL: InterVarsity, 1996), 114.
[5] Philip Turner, "The Powerlessness of Talking Heads: Re-Evangelization in a Postmodern World—The Place of Ethics," in *The Strange New Word of the Gospel,* 83.
[6] Ibid., 83-84.
[7] Walter Thomas Conner, *The Cross in the New Testament* (Nashville: Broadman, 1954), 96.
[8] Cecil Stalnaker, "WDJS—What Does Jesus Say . . . About Receptivity," in *The Centrality of Christ in Contemporary Missions,* ed. Mike Barnett and Mike Pocock (Pasadena: William Carey Library, 2005), 221, 222.
[9] David E. Bjork, "The Future of Christianity in Western Europe," *Missiology* (July 2006): 317.
[10] John MacArthur, *Twelve Ordinary Men: How the Master Shaped His Disciples for Greatness, and What He Wants to Do with You* (Nashville: W Publishing Group, 2002), 156.

[11] Ibid., 164. See also, Ruth A. Tucker, *From Jerusalem to Irian Jaya: A Biographical History of Christian Missions* (Grand Rapids: Acadamie, 1983), 29.
[12] J. Herbert Kane, *A Global View of Christian Missions: From Pentecost to the Present,* revised ed. (Grand Rapids: Baker, 1985), 108.
[13] Elmer L. Towns and Ed Stetzer, *Perimeters of Light: Biblical Boundaries for the Emerging Church* (Chicago: Moody, 2004), 147.
[14] Ibid., 134-35.
[15] J. Isamu Yamamoto, *Beyond Buddhism* (Downers Grove, IL: InterVarsity, 1982), 117.
[16] Ibid., 109.
[17] *Theological Dictionary of the New Testament,* Abridged ed., 1985, s. v. "Metanoia," by J. Behm.
[18] Leah Coulter, *Rediscovering the Power of Repentance and Forgiveness* (Atlanta: Ampelon, 2006), 71-74.
[19] David J. Hesselgrave, *Communicating Christ Cross-Culturally: An Introduction to Missionary Communication* (Grand Rapids: Academie, 1978), 191.
[20] Ibid., 191-93.
[21] Ramachandra, 41.
[22] Dallas Willard, *The Spirit of the Disciplines: Understanding How God Changes Lives* (San Francisco: HarperCollins, 1988), 67.
[23] Ibid., 68.
[24] Waylon B. Moore, *Multiplying Disciples: The New Testament Method for Church Growth* (Tampa: Missions Unlimited, 1981), 23.
[25] Tucker, 114-21.
[26] Heim, 130, 131.
[27] Lenski, 628.
[28] Ibid., 631.
[29] Arthur, 300, sees the power of the keys as our exercising authority on behalf of Christ to free people from the powers of evil. The most traditional view of "whatever" is that it refers to sanctioning or permitting certain behavior as moral rather than as immoral.
[30] C. S. Lewis, *Surprised by Joy: The Shape of My Early Life* (New York: Harcourt Brace Jovanovich, 1955), 236, 237.
[31] Francis Schaeffer, *The God Who Is There,* in *The Complete Works of Francis Schaeffer,* Vol. 1, *A Christian View of Philosophy and Culture* (Westchester, IL: Crossway, 1982), 146.
[32] Tony Carnes, "New York's Hope," *Christianity Today* (December 2004): 33, 34.
[33] Ibid., 34, 35.
[34] Ibid., 34, 35, 37.
[35] Towns and Stetzer, 17.

Chapter Three

[1] Turner, 82-83.
[2] Ibid., 80.
[3] Donald Bloesch, *A Theology of Word and Spirit: Authority and Method in Theology* (Downers Grove, IL: InterVarsity, 1992), 136.
[4] James F. Engel and William A.Dyrness, *Changing the Mind of Missions: Where Have We Gone Wrong?* (Downers Grove, IL: InterVarsity, 2000), 21.
[5] Ibid., 22.
[6] Philip Edgcumbe Hughes, *Hebrews* (Grand Rapids: Eerdmans, 1977), 228.
[7] Willard, 17.
[8] Ronald Allen and Gordon Borror, *Worship: Recovering the Missing Jewel* (Eugene: Wipf and Stock, 2000), 24.
[9] Roger E. Olson, *The Christian Story: Twenty Centuries of Tradition and Reform* (Downers Grove, IL: InterVarsity, 1999), 38-39.
[10] Engel and Dyrness, 66.
[11] Anderson, *Victory over the Darkness,* 54.
[12] Arnold, *Powers of Darkness,* 19.
[13] Ibid., 122-23.
[14] John Dawson, "The Seventh Time Around: Breaking through a City's Invisible Barriers to the Gospel," in *Territorial Spirits: Insights on Strategic-Level Spiritual Warfare from Nineteen Christian Leaders,* ed. C. Peter Wagner (Chichester, England: Sovereign World Limited, 1991), 138.
[15] Sally Morgenthaler, *Worship Evangelism: Inviting Unbelievers into the Presence of God* (Grand Rapids: Zondervan, 1995), 49.
[16] Allen and Borror, 102-03.
[17] Dan Kimball, *The Emerging Church: Vintage Christianity for New Generations* (Grand Rapids: Zondervan, 2003), 114.
[18] Morgenthaler, 39.
[19] Victor C. Pfitzer, *Hebrews* (Nashville: Abingdom, 1997), 84.
[20] Simon J. Kistemaker, *Hebrews* (Grand Rapids: Eerdmans, 1984), 116; Paul Ellingsworth, *Hebrews* (Grand Rapids: Eerdmans, 1993), 260-61.
[21] William Manson, *Hebrews* (London: Hodder and Stoughton, 1951), 56-58.
[22] Philip Edgcumbe Hughes, *Revelation* (Grand Rapids: Eerdmans, 1990), 203-08.
[23] John Newport, *The Lion and the Lamb: A Commentary on the Book of Revelation for Today* (Nashville: Broadman, 1986), 287-88.
[24] Ellingsworth, 261.
[25] William R. Newell, *Hebrews* (Iowa Falls, IA: World Bible Publishers, 1947), 136.
[26] Dean Flemming, *Contextualization in the New Testament: Patterns for Theology and Mission* (Downers Grove, IL: InterVarsity, 2005), 198.
[27] Paul G. Hiebert and Eloise Hiebert Meneses, *Incarnational Ministry: Planting Churches in Band, Tribal, Peasant and Urban Societies* (Grand Rapids: Baker Books, 1995), 41.

[28] Darrow L. Miller, *Discipling Nations: The Power of Truth to Transform Cultures* (Seattle: YWAM Publishing, 1998), 39.
[29] Ibid, 68.
[30] Hesselgrave, 142.
[31] Ibid, 143.
[32] Hiebert, 42.

Chapter Four

[1] George Gallup, Jr., and William Paul McKay, "The Changing Face of Japan." Presented to the Japan Evangelical Missionary Association Mission Leadership Consultation, Tokyo, Japan, February 19, 2006.
[2] George Gallup, Jr., *Spread the Gospel in Japan: Severe Challenges but Exciting Opportunities,* p. 8, presented to the Japan Evangelical Missionary Association Leadership Consultation, Tokyo, Japan, February 19, 2006.
[3] *World Christian Database,* for example, shows over 550 million Christians among a population 725 million in Europe. http://www.worldchristiandatabase.org/wcd/esweb.asp?WCI=Results&Query=425, accessed April 13, 2006.
[4] Martin Robinson and Dwight Smith, *Invading Secular Space: Strategies for Tomorrow's Church* (Mill Hill, UK: Monarch, 2003), 20.
[5] Ibid., 21.
[6] Daniele Hervieu-Leger, *Catholicisme, la fin d'un monde* (Paris: Bayard, 2003), 97; cited in Bjork, 309.
[7] Bjork, 309, 313.
[8] Carl E. Braaten, "The Future of the Apostolic Imperative: At the Crossroads of World Evangelization," in *The Strange New Word of the Gospel,* 160-61.
[9] The 10-40 Window is the area of the earth's eastern hemisphere, defined on the south by 10 degrees latitude south and of the north by 40 degrees latitude north, in which most people who have never heard the Gospel live. Many of these people live in the traditional Muslim, Hindu and Buddhist nations of South Asia and North Africa.
[10] Timothy George and John Woodbridge, *The Mark of Jesus: Loving in a Way the World Can See* (Chicago: Moody, 2005), 23.
[11] William L. Banks, *In Search of the Great Commission: What Did Jesus Really Say?* (Chicago: Moody, 1991), 13, 16-17.
[12] Ibid., 39-41.
[13] Green, 208.
[14] Ibid., 211-13.
[15] Ibid., 300-55.
[16] Ibid., 243.
[17] Banks, 45-46.

[18] Erwin W. Lutzer, *Christ among Other Gods: A Defense of Christ in an Age of Tolerance* (Chicago: Moody, 1994), 205.
[19] Ibid., 52.
[20] Stephen J. Wellum, "The Means of Grace: Baptism," in *The Compromised Church,* ed. John H. Armstrong (Wheaton, IL: Crossway, 1998), 154, 155.
[21] Ibid., 151.
[22] James D. G. Dunn, *Baptism in the Holy Spirit* (Philadelphia: Westminster, 1970), 226-28.
[23] Andreas J. Kostenberger and Peter T. O'Brien, *Salvation to the Ends of the Earth: A Biblical Theology of Mission* (Downers Grove, IL: InterVarsity, 2001), 222.
[24] George and Woodbridge, 154.
[25] Francis Schaeffer, *The Mark of the Christian* (L'Abri Fellowship, 1970), 29; quoted in George and Woodbridge, 48.
[26] George and Woodbridge, 52-53.
[27] Green, 256.
[28] Rodney Stark, *The Rise of Christianity: How the Obscure, Marginal Jesus Movement Became the Dominant Religious Force in the Western World in a Few Centuries* (San Francisco: Harper Collins, 1997), 73-94.
[29] Anderson, *Victory over the Darkness,* 236.
[30] Banks, 101.
[31] Millard J. Erickson, *Christian Theology,* Vol. 3 (Grand Rapids: Baker, 1985), 936.
[32] Ibid., 936-37.
[33] Banks, 108.
[34] Ibid.
[35] Arnold, *Three Crucial Questions,* 165.
[36] Arthur, 167.
[37] Banks, 74.
[38] Lenski, 1171.
[39] Banks, 72-73.
[40] Ibid., 78-80.
[41] Edward R. Dayton, "To Reach the Unreached," in *Perspectives on the World Christian Movement,* ed. Ralph D. Winter and Stephen C. Hawthorne (Pasadena: William Carey Library, 1981), 586-87, defines a people as "a significantly large sociological grouping of individuals who perceive themselves to have a common affinity for one another because of their shared language, religion, ethnicity, residence, occupation, class or caste, situation, etc., or combinations of these."
[42] Banks, 75-76.
[43] Ibid., 76-77.
[44] Bill Hull, *The Disciple-Making Church* (Grand Rapids: Fleming H. Revell, 1990), 21.
[45] Kevin Giles, *What on Earth Is the Church? An Exploration in New Testament Theology* (Downers Grove, IL: InterVarsity, 1995), 122-23.
[46] Wellum, 151.

[47] Ibid.
[48] Moore, 42.
[49] Banks, 81.
[50] Hull, 21-22.
[51] Moore, 21-23.
[52] John Stott, *The Spirit, the Church, and the World* (Downers Grove, IL: InterVarsity, 1990), 41-42.
[53] Peter P. J. Beyerhaus, *God's Kingdom and the Utopian Error: Discerning the Biblical Kingdom of God from Its Political Counterfeits* (Wheaton, IL: Crossway, 1992), 90-91.
[54] Ibid., 26-27.
[55] Ibid., 30-31.
[56] Banks, 120.
[57] Oscar Cullmann, *The Christology of the New Testament,* trans. by Shirley C. Guthrie and Charles A. M. Hall, rev. ed. (Philadelphia: Westminster, 1963), 320, 321.
[58] Gordon D. Fee, *God's Empowering Presence: The Holy Spirit in the Letters of Paul* (Peabody, MA: Hendrickson, 1994), 843-45.
[59] Ibid., 845.
[60] Banks, 128-29.
[61] Stott, 40.
[62] Banks, 134-35.
[63] Hull, 9.
[64] Ibid., 11.
[65] Ibid., 13.
[66] Moore, 15,
[67] Brother Yun and Paul Hattaway, *The Heavenly Man* (Carlisle, UK: Piquant, 2003), 285.
[68] Robinson and Smith, 209-10.

Chapter Five

[1] Dunn, 44-47.
[2] Arturo G. Azurdia, III, "Preaching: The Decisive Function," in *The Compromised Church,* ed. John H. Armstrong (Wheaton: Crossway, 1998), 206.
[3] Stott, 62.
[4] Walter Thomas Conner, *The Work of the Holy Spirit* (Nashville: Broadman, 1940), 63.
[5] Ibid., 62.
[6] Ben Witherington, III, *The Acts of the Apostles: A Socio-Rhetorical Commentary* (Grand Rapids: Eerdmans, 1998), 175.
[7] C. Peter Wagner, *Spreading the Fire: A New Look at Acts—God's Training for Every Christian* (Ventura, CA: Regal, 1994), 116-18.

---

[8] Stott, 91-95.
[9] Dennis E. Johnson, *The Message of Acts* (Phillipsburg, NJ: P & R, 1997), 65-66.
[10] Ibid., 204-05.
[11] French L. Arrington, *Acts* (Peabody, MA: Hendrickson, 1988), 48.
[12] Ibid., 161-62.
[13] Witherington, 299.
[14] Stott, 78.
[15] Ibid., 68.
[16] Howard Clark Kee, *Good News to the Ends of the Earth* (London: SCM, 1990), 31-32.
[17] Stott, 189.
[18] David Lertis Matson, *Household Conversion Narratives in Acts* (Sheffield, English: Sheffield Academic, 1996), 107-08.
[19] Witherington, 358.
[20] Dunn, 80-82.
[21] Witherington, 358.
[22] George and Woodbridge, 91, 92.
[23] Johnson, 133.
[24] Stott, 192.
[25] Stott, 192.
[26] Johnson, 137.
[27] Joanne Shetler and Patricia Purvis, *And the Word Came with Power* (Orlando: Wycliffe, 1992), 32.
[28] Ibid., 45-49.
[29] Ibid., 54.
[30] Ibid., 85-87.
[31] Ibid., 102.
[32] Ibid., 120.
[33] Joel B. Green, "Salvation to the End of the Earth: God as Savior in the Acts of the Apostles," in *Witness to the Gospel: The Theology of Acts,* eds. I. Howard Marshall and David Peterson (Grand Rapids: Eerdmans, 1998), 94-95.
[34] Hull, 99.
[35] Garrett, 66.
[36] Ibid., 67.
[37] Johnson, 170-71.
[38] Garrett, 70.
[39] Johnson, 171.
[40] Garrett, 72.
[41] Unger, 116-17.
[42] Witherington, 396.
[43] C. Peter Wagner, *Lighting the World: Acts of the Holy Spirit,* Vol. 2 (Ventura, CA: Regal, 1995), 154-57; Arnold, *Powers of Darkness,* 32.
[44] Garrett, 81.
[45] Arnold, *Three Crucial Questions,* 167.

[46] Unger, 140.
[47] C. Peter Wagner, *Blazing the Way: Acts of the Holy Spirit,* Vol. 3 (Ventura, CA: Regal, 1995), 72; Unger, 141-42.
[48] Witherington, 494-95.
[49] Johnson, 177; Wagner, *Blazing the Way,* 73.
[50] Stott, 264.
[51] Wagner, *Blazing the Way,* 74-75.
[52] Johnson, 178.
[53] Wagner, *Blazing the Way,* 77-78.
[54] Ibid., 79-81.
[55] Yun and Hattaway, 241-60.
[56] Green, "Salvation to the Ends of the Earth," 103.
[57] Matson,162.
[58] Ibid., 162-64.
[59] Stott, *Spirit, Church and World,* 267-68.
[60] Ibid., 277.
[61] Ibid.; Wagner, *Blazing the Way,* 101.
[62] Arnold, *Powers of Darkness,* 35-45.
[63] Ibid., 35-36.
[64] John Milbank, "The Gospel of Affinity," in *The Strange New Word of the Gospel,* 7.
[65] Arrington, 179-80.
[66] Stott, 284-88.
[67] Witherington, 575-76.
[68] Johnson, 180.
[69] Arnold, *Three Crucial Questions,* 91.
[70] Garrett, 91.
[71] Ibid., 92-94.
[72] Unger, 105.
[73] Arnold, *Three Crucial Questions,* 91; Garrett, 95-96.
[74] Johnson, 181-82.
[75] Conner, *The Work of the Holy Spirit,* 65-67.
[76] Ibid., 64-67.
[77] Stott, 202-03.
[78] Wagner, *Lighting the World, 92*-103.
[79] Michael Green, *I Believe in the Holy Spirit* (Grand Rapids: Eerdmans, 1980), 68-74.
[80] R. A. Torrey, *The Holy Spirit* (n. p. : Revell, 1927), 51.
[81] Hull, 62-75.
[82] Ibid., 175.
[83] Bill M. Easum and Thomas G. Bandy, *Growing Spiritual Redwoods* (Nashville: Abingdon, 1997), 30.

Chapter Six

[1] Philip Jenkins, *The Next Christendom: The Coming of Global Christianity* (New York: Oxford, 2007), 80-84.
[2] Michael Pocock, Gailyn Van Rheenen and Douglas McConnell, *The Changing Face of World Missions* (Grand Rapids: Baker Academic, 2005), 134-35.
[3] Jenkins, 2-3.
[4] Pocock, Van Rheenen and McConnell, 142.
[5] Michael T. Cooper, "Post-Constantinian Missions: Lessons from the Resurgence of Paganism," in *Contextualization and Syncretism,* ed. Gailyn Van Rheenen (Pasadena: William Carey Library, 2006), 193.
[6] Ibid, 179-98.
[7] Wade Clark Roof, *Spiritual Marketplace: Baby Boomers and the Remaking of American Religion* (Princeton: Princeton University Press, 1999), 8-10.
[8] Ibid, 189.
[9] Easum, *Leadership on the Other Side,* 160.
[10] Ibid, 72-73.
[11] Randy Frazee, *The Connecting Church* (Grand Rapids: Zondervan, 2001), 35-37.
[12] Easum, *Leadership of the Other Side,* 75-79.
[13] Thomas D. Lea and Hayne P. Griffin, Jr., *1,2 Timothy, Titus,* The New American Commentary, Vol. 34 (Nashville: Broadman, 1992), 238.
[14] Hull, 172-74.
[15] Lea and Griffin, 236.
[16] Donald G. Bloesch, *Holy Scripture* (Downers Grove, IL: InterVarsity, 1994), 58.
[17] Ibid, 55.
[18] Lea and Griffin, 234.
[19] Ronald A. Ward, *Commentary on 1& 2 Timothy, Titus* (Waco: Word, 1974), 199.
[20] Hull, 175.
[21] Lea and Griffin, 237.
[22] Hull, 177, 178.
[23] Donald Guthrie, *The Pastoral Epistles,* Tyndale New Testament Commentaries (Leicester, England: InterVarsity, 1984), 165.
[24] Hull, 175.
[25] Frazee, 71.
[26] Ibid, 85.
[27] Easum and Bandy, 150.
[28] The following discussion is based on Frazee, 119-36.
[29] Paul D. Stanley and J. Robert Clinton, *Connecting: The Mentoring Relationships You Need to Succeed in Life* (Colorado Springs: NavPress, 1992), 33.
[30] Ibid, 43-44.
[31] Ibid, 57.
[32] Ibid, 215-24.
[33] John MacArthur, *Keys to Spiritual Growth* (Grand Rapids: Fleming H. Revell, 1976), 98, 99.

[34] Richard J. Foster, *The Celebration of Discipline* (San Francisco: Harper San Francisco, 1978),152.
[35] Ibid, 146-49.
[36] Willard, 187-88.
[37] Ibid, 187.
[38] Howard A. Snyder, *Community of the King* (Downers Grove, IL: InterVarsity, 1977), 101.
[39] Ibid, 102-03.
[40] Michael Frost and Alan Hirsch, *The Shaping of Things to Come* (Peabody, MA: Hendrickson, 2003), 145.
[41] Snyder, *Community of the King,* 115.
[42] Howard A. Snyder, *Radical Renewal: The Problem of Wineskins Today* (Houston: Touch Publications, 1996), 139.
[43] Ibid, 141-42.
[44] Life Transformation Groups, or LTG's, have been used to encouraged spiritual growth in a variety of settings. For more information, see Neil Cole, *Cultivating a Life for God* (St. Charles, IL: Church Smart Resources, 1999).
[45] Snyder, *Community of the King,* 146, 147.
[46] Ibid, 156.
[47] Ed Stetzer, *Planting New Churches in a Postmodern Age* (Nashville: Broadman and Holman, 2003), 193.
[48] Malone, 118.

SOURCES

Alleine, Richard. *The World Conquered by the Faithful Christian,* reprint. Morgan, PA: Soli Deo Gloria, 1995.

Allen, Ronald, and Gordon Borror. *Worship: Recovering the Missing Jewel.* Eugene: Wipf and Stock, 2000.

Anderson, Neil T. *The Bondage Breaker.* Eugene, OR: Harvest House, 1993.

_____. *Victory over the Darkness: Realizing the Power of Your Identity in Christ.* Ventura, CA: Regal, 1990.

Armstrong, John H, ed. *The Coming Evangelical Crisis*. Chicago: Moody, 1996.

_____, ed. *The Compromised Church.* Wheaton, IL: Crossway, 1998.

Arnold, Clinton. *Powers of Darkness: Principalities and Powers in Paul's Letters.* Downers Grove, IL: InterVarsity, 1992.

_____. *Three Crucial Questions about Spiritual Warfare.* Grand Rapids: Baker, 1997.

Arrington, French L. *Acts.* Peabody, MA: Hendrickson, 1988.

Arthur, Kay. *Lord, Is It Warfare? Teach Me to Stand.* Sisters, OR: Multnomah, 1991.

Banks, William L. *In Search of the Great Commission: What Did Jesus Really Say?* (Chicago: Moody, 1991.

Barnett, Mike, and Michael Pocock, ed. *The Centrality of Christ in Contemporary Missions.* Evangelical Missiological Society Series. Pasadena: William Carey Library, 2005.

Beyerhaus, Peter P. J. *God's Kingdom and the Utopian Error: Discerning the Biblical Kingdom of God from Its Political Counterfeits.* Wheaton, IL: Crossway, 1992.

Bjork, David E. "The Future of Christianity in Western Europe."*Missiology* (July 2006): 309-24.

Bloesch, Donald G. *A Theology of Word and Spirit: Authority and Method in Theology.* Downers Grove, IL: InterVarsity, 1992.

_____. *Holy Scripture.* Downers Grove, IL: InterVarsity, 1994.

_____. *Jesus Christ: Savior and Lord.* Downers Grove, IL: InterVarsity, 1997.

Boyd, Gregory A. *God at War: The Bible & Spiritual Conflict.* Downers Grove, IL: InterVarsity, 1997.

_____. *Satan and the Problem of Evil: Constructing a Trinitarian Warfare Theodicy.* Downers Grove, IL: InterVarsity, 2001.

Braaten, Carl E., and Robert W. Jansen, ed. *The Strange New Word of the Gospel: Re-Evangelizing in the Postmodern World.* Grand Rapids: Eerdmans, 2002.

Carnes, Tony. "New York's Hope." *Christianity Today* (December 2004): 33, 34.

Cole, Neil. *Cultivating a Life for God.* St. Charles, IL: Church Smart Resources, 1999.

Conner, Walter Thomas. *The Cross in the New Testament.* Nashville: Broadman, 1954.

_____. *The Work of the Holy Spirit.* Nashville: Broadman, 1940.

Coulter, Leah. *Rediscovering the Power of Repentance and Forgiveness.* Atlanta: Ampelon, 2006.

Cullmann, Oscar. *The Christology of the New Testament.* Trans. By Shirley C. Guthrie and Charles A. M. Hall, rev. ed. Philadelphia:Westminster, 1963.

Dunn, James D. G. *Baptism in the Holy Spirit.* Philadelphia: Westminster, 1970.

Easum, Bill M. *Leadership on the Other Side: No Rules, Just Clues.* Nashville: Abingdon, 2000.

Easum, Bill M., and Thomas G. Bandy. *Growing Spiritual Redwoods.* Nashville: Abingdon, 1997.

Ellingsworth, Paul. *Hebrews.* Grand Rapids: Eerdmans, 1993.

Engel, James F., and William A.Dyrness, *Changing the Mind of Missions: Where Have We Gone Wrong?* Downers Grove, IL: InterVarsity, 2000.

Erickson, Millard J. *Christian Theology.* Grand Rapids: Baker, 1985.

Fee, Gordon D. *God's Empowering Presence: The Holy Spirit in the Letters of Paul.* Peabody, MA: Hendrickson, 1994.

Flemming, Dean. *Contextualization in the New Testament: Patterns for Theology and Mission.* Downers Grove, IL: InterVarsity, 2005.

Foster, Richard J. *The Celebration of Discipline.* San Francisco: Harper San Francisco, 1978.

Frazee, Randy. *The Connecting Church: Beyond Small Groups to Authentic Community.* Grand Rapids: Zondervan, 2001.

Frost, Michael, and Alan Hirsch. *The Shaping of Things to Come.* Peabody, MA: Hendrickson, 2003.

Gallup, George, Jr. *Spread the Gospel in Japan: Severe Challenges but Exciting Opportunities.* Presented to the Japan Evangelical Missionary Association Leadership Consultation, Tokyo, Japan, February 19,2006.

Gallup, George, Jr., and William Paul McKay. "The Changing Face of Japan." Presented to the Japan Evangelical Missionary Association Mission Leadership Consultation, Tokyo, Japan,February 19, 2006.

Garrett, Susan R. *The Demise of the Devil.* Minneapolis: Fortress, 1989.

George, Timothy, and John Woodbridge. *The Mark of Jesus: Loving in a Way the World Can See.* Chicago: Moody, 2005.

Giles, Kent. *What on Earth Is the Church? An Exploration in New Testament Theology.* Downers Grove, IL: InterVarsity, 1995.

Godet, Frederic Louis. *Commentary on John's Gospel.* Grand Rapids: Kregel, 1978.

Green, Michael. *Evangelism in the Early Church,* revised ed. Grand Rapids: Eerdmans, 2003.

_____. *I Believe in the Holy Spirit.* Grand Rapids: Eerdmans, 1980.

Groothius, Douglas. *Truth Decay: Defending Christianity against the Challenges of Postmodernism.* Downers Grove, IL: InterVarsity, 2000.

Guthrie, Donald. *The Pastoral Epistles.* Tyndale New Testament Commentaries. Leicester, England: InterVarsity, 1984.

Heim, S. Mark. *Is Christ the Only Way: Christian Faith in a Pluralistic World.* Valley Forge, PA: Judson, 1985.

Hendriksen, William. *Luke.* Grand Rapids: Baker, 1978.

Hesselgrave, David J. *Communicating Christ Cross-Culturally: An Introduction to Missionary Communication.* Grand Rapids: Academie, 1978.

Hiebert, Paul G., and Eloise Hiebert Meneses. *Incarnational Ministry: Planting Churches in Band, Tribal, Peasant and Urban Societies.* Grand Rapids: Baker Books, 1995.

Hughes, Philip Edgcumbe. *Hebrews.* Grand Rapids: Eerdmans, 1977.

_____. *Revelation.* Grand Rapids: Eerdmans, 1990.

Hull, Bill. *The Disciple-Making Church.* Grand Rapids: Fleming H. Revell, 1990.

Hunt, Boyd. *Redeemed! Eschatological Redemption and the Kingdom of God.* Nashville: Broadman and Holman, 1993.

Jenkins, Philip. *The Next Christendom: The Coming of Global Christianity.* New York: Oxford, 2007.

Johnson, Dennis E. *The Message of Acts.* Phillipsburg, NJ: P & R, 1997.

Johnson, Philip. *The Wedge of Truth: Splitting the Foundations of Naturalism.* Downers Grove, IL: InterVarsity, 2000.

Kane, J. Herbert. *A Global View of Christian Missions: From Pentecost to the Present,* revised ed. Grand Rapids: Baker, 1985.

Kee, Howard Clark. *Good News to the Ends of the Earth.* London: SCM, 1990.

Kimball, Charles A. *Jesus' Exposition of the Old Testament in Luke's Gospel.* Sheffield, England: JSOT, 1994.

Kimball, Dan. *The Emerging Church: Vintage Christianity for New Generations.* Grand Rapids: Zondervan, 2003.

Kistemaker, Simon J. *Hebrews.* Grand Rapids: Eerdmans, 1984.

Kostenberger, Andreas J., and Peter T. O'Brien. *Salvation to the Ends of the Earth: A Biblical Theology of Mission.* Downers Grove, IL: InterVarsity, 2001.

Lea, Thomas D., and Hayne P. Griffin, Jr., *1,2 Timothy, Titus.* The New American Commentary, Vol. 34. Nashville: Broadman, 1992.

Lenski, R. C. H. *Matthew.* Grand Rapids: Baker, 1973.

Lewis, C. S. *Surprised by Joy: The Shape of My Early Life.* New York: Harcourt Brace Jovanovich, 1955.

Lightner, Robert. *Angels, Satan and Demons.* Nashville: Word, 1998.

Lindars, Barnabas. *The Gospel of John.* New Century Bible Commentary, Ronald E.Clements and Matthew Black, eds. Grand Rapids: Eerdmans, 1972.

Lutzer, Erwin W. *Christ among Other Gods: A Defense of Christ in an Age of Tolerance.* Chicago: Moody, 1994.

MacArthur, John. *Keys to Spiritual Growth.* Grand Rapids: Fleming H. Revell, 1976.

_____. *Twelve Ordinary Men: How the Master Shaped His Disciples for Greatness, and What He Wants to Do with You.* Nashville: W Publishing Group, 2002.

Malone, Kelly. *Hearing Christ's Voice: Living and Proclaiming the Gospel in an Embattled World.* Garland, TX: Hannibal, 2006.

Manson, William. *Hebrews.* London: Hodder and Stoughton, 1951.

Marshall, I. Howard, and David Peterson, ed. *Witness to the Gospel: The Theology of Acts.* Grand Rapids: Eerdmans, 1998.

Matson, David Lertis. *Household Conversion Narratives in Acts.* Sheffield, English: Sheffield Academic, 1996.

Miller, Darrow L. *Discipling Nations: The Power of Truth to Transform Cultures.* Seattle: YWAM Publishing, 1998.

Moore, Waylon B. *Multiplying Disciples: The New Testament Method for Church Growth.* Tampa: Missions Unlimited, 1981.

Morgenthaler, Sally. *Worship Evangelism: Inviting Unbelievers into the Presence of God.* Grand Rapids: Zondervan, 1995.

Morris, Leon. *The Gospel according to John.* The New International Commentary on the New Testament, F. F. Bruce, ed. Grand Rapids: Eerdmans, 1971.

Newell, William R. *Hebrews.* Iowa Falls, IA: World Bible Publishers, 1947.

Newport, John. *The Lion and the Lamb: A Commentary on the Book of Revelation for Today.* Nashville: Broadman, 1986.

Noll, Stephen F. *Angels of Light, Powers of Darkness: Thinking Biblically about Angels, Satan & Principalities.* Downers Grove, IL: InterVarsity, 1998.

Olson, Roger E. *The Christian Story: Twenty Centuries of Tradition and Reform.* Downers Grove, IL: InterVarsity, 1999.

Page, Sydney H. T. *Powers of Evil: A Biblical Study of Satan and Demons.* Grand Rapids: Baker, 1995.

Pfitzer, Victor C. *Hebrews.* Nashville: Abingdon, 1997.

Pocock, Michael, Gailyn Van Rheenen and Douglas McConnell. *The Changing Face of World Missions.* Grand Rapids: Baker Academic, 2005.

Powlinson, David. *Power Encounters.* Grand Rapids: Baker, 1995.

Ramachandra, Vinoth. *Gods that Fail: Modern Idolatry and Christian Mission.* Downers Grove, IL: InterVarsity, 1996.

Robinson, Martin, and Dwight Smith. *Invading Secular Space: Strategies for Tomorrow's Church.* Mill Hill, UK: Monarch, 2003.

Roof, Wade Clark. *Spiritual Marketplace: Baby Boomers and the Remaking of American Religion.* Princeton: Princeton University Press, 1999.

Schaeffer, Francis. *The God Who Is There.* In *The Complete Works of Francis Schaeffer,* Vol. 1, *A Christian View of Philosophy and Culture.* Westchester, IL: Crossway, 1982.

Shetler, Joanne, and Patricia Purvis. *And the Word Came with Power.* Orlando: Wycliffe, 1992.

Snyder, Howard A. *Community of the King.* Downers Grove, IL: InterVarsity, 1977.

_____. *Radical Renewal: The Problem of Wineskins Today.* Houston: Touch Publications, 1996.

Stanley, Paul D., and J. Robert Clinton. *Connecting: The Mentoring Relationships You Need to Succeed in Life.* Colorado Springs: NavPress, 1992.

Stark, Rodney. *The Rise of Christianity: How the Obscure, Marginal Jesus Movement Became the Dominant Religious Force in the Western World in a Few Centuries.* San Francisco: Harper Collins, 1997.

Stetzer, Ed. *Planting New Churches in a Postmodern Age.* Nashville: Broadman and Holman, 2003.

Stott, John. *The Spirit, the Church, and the World.* Downers Grove, IL: InterVarsity, 1990.

Tannehill, Robert C. *Luke.* Nashville: Abingdon, 1995.

Theological Dictionary of the New Testament, Abridged ed., 1985.

Torrey, R. A. *The Holy Spirit.* n. p. : Revell, 1927.

Towns, Elmer L., and Ed Stetzer. *Perimeters of Light: Biblical Boundaries for the Emerging Church.* Chicago: Moody, 2004.

Tucker, Ruth A. *From Jerusalem to Irian Jaya: A Biographical History of Christian Missions.* Grand Rapids: Acadamie, 1983.

Unger, Merrill F. *Biblical Demonology: A Study of Spiritual Forces at Work Today.* Grand Rapids: Kregel, 1994.

Van Rheenen, Gailyn, ed. *Contextualization and Syncretism.* ed. Pasadena: William Carey Library, 2006.

Wagner, C. Peter. *Blazing the Way: Acts of the Holy Spirit,* Vol. 3. Ventura, CA: Regal, 1995.

_____. *Lighting the World: Acts of the Holy Spirit,* Vol. 2. Ventura, CA: Regal, 1995.

_____. *Spreading the Fire: A New Look at Acts—God's Training for Every Christian.* Ventura, CA: Regal, 1994.

_____, ed. *Territorial Spirits: Insights on Strategic-Level Spiritual Warfare from Nineteen Christian Leaders.* Chichester, England: Sovereign World Limited, 1991.

Ward, Ronald A. *Commentary on 1& 2 Timothy, Titus.* Waco: Word, 1974.

Warner, Timothy M. *Spiritual Warfare: Victory over the Powers of This Dark World.* Wheaton: Crossway, 1991.

Willard, Dallas. *The Spirit of the Disciplines: Understanding How God Changes Lives.* San Francisco: HarperCollins, 1988.

Winter, Ralph D., and Stephen C. Hawthorne, ed. *Perspectives on the World Christian Movement.* Pasadena: William Carey Library, 1981.

Witherington, Ben, III. *The Acts of the Apostles: A Socio-Rhetorical Commentary.* Grand Rapids: Eerdmans, 1998.

World Christian Database. http://www.worldchristiandatabase.org/wcd/esweb.asp?WCI=Results&Query=425, accessed April 13, 2006.

Wright, Tom. *Bringing the Church to the World: Renewing the Church to Confront Paganism Entrenched in Western Culture.* Minneapolis: Bethany House, 1992.

Yamamoto, J. Isamu. *Beyond Buddhism.* Downers Grove, IL: InterVarsity, 1982.

Yun, Brother, and Paul Hattaway. *The Heavenly Man*. Carlisle, UK: Piquant, 2003.

Zacharias, Bryan G. *The Embattled Christian: William Gurnall and the Puritan View of Spiritual Warfare.* Carlisle, PA: Banner of Truth, 1995.

CPSIA information can be obtained at www.ICGtesting.com
Printed in the USA
LVOW030626301211

261641LV00006B/53/P